GUINEA WOMAN

LORNA GOODISON

GUINEA WOMAN

New and Selected Poems

CARCANET

First published in 2000 by
Carcanet Press Limited
4th Floor, Conavon Court
12-16 Blackfriars Street
Manchester M3 5BQ

A CIP catalogue record for this book
is available from the British Library
ISBN 85754 486 2

The publisher acknowledges financial assistance
from the Arts Council of England

Set in 10pt Palatino by Bryan Williamson, Frome
Printed and bound in England by SRP Ltd, Exeter

Contents

The poems on pp. 11–28 previously appeared in *I Am Becoming My Mother*, and those on pp. 30–38 in *Heartease*, both published by New Beacon Books and reprinted with permission.

The Road of the Dread

That dey road no pave
like any other black-face road
it no have no definite color
and it fence two side
with live barbwire.

And no look fi no milepost
fi measure you walking
and no tek no stone as
dead or familiar

for sometime you pass a ting
you know as . . . call it stone again
and is a snake ready fi squeeze yu
kill yu
or is a dead man tek him
possessions tease yu.

Then the place dem yu feel
is resting place because time
before that yu welcome like rain,
go dey again?

bad dawg, bad face tun fi drive yu underground
wey yu no have no light fi walk
and yu find sey that many yu meet who sey
them understand
is only from dem mout dem talk.

One good ting though, that same treatment
mek yu walk untold distance
for to continue yu have fe walk far
away from the wicked.

Pan dis same road ya sista
sometime yu drink yu salt sweat fi water
for yu sure sey at least dat no pisen,
and bread? yu picture it and chew it accordingly
and some time yu surprise fi know how dat full
man belly.

Some day no have no definite color
no beginning and no ending, it just name day
or night as how you feel fi call it.

Den why I tread it brother?
well mek I tell yu bout the day dem
when the father send some little bird
that swallow flute fi trill me
and when him instruct the sun fi smile pan me first.

And the sky calm like sea when it sleep
and a breeze like a laugh follow mi.
Or the man find a stream that pure like baby mind
and the water ease down yu throat
and quiet yu inside.

And better still when yu meet another traveler
who have flour and yu have water and man and man
make bread together.
And dem time dey the road run straight and sure
like a young horse that cant tire
and yu catch a glimpse of the end
through the water in yu eye
I wont tell yu what I spy
but is fi dat alone I tread this road.

Tamarind Season

The skin atrophies
to a case of spinster brown.

The soft welcome within
needs protecting
so she grows wasp-waisted
again
wasp-waisted

The welcome turns sour
she finds a woman's tongue
and clacks curses at the wind
for taking advantage.

Box her about this way
and that is the reason.

Wait is the reason.

Tamarind Season.

Jamaica 1980

It trails always behind me
a webbed seine with a catch of fantasy
a penance I pay for being me
who took the order of poetry.
Always there with the gaping holes
and the mended ones, and the stand-in words.
But this time my Jamaica
my green-clad muse
this time your callings are of no use.
I am spied on by your mountains
wire-tapped by your secret streams
your trees dripping blood-leaves
and jasmine selling tourist-dreams.

For over all this edenism
hangs the smell of necromancy
and each man eats his brother's flesh
Lord, so much of the cannibal left
in the jungle of my people's tongues.

We've sacrificed babies
and burnt our mothers
as payment to some viridian-eyed God dread
who works in cocaine under hungry men's heads.

And mine the task of writing it down
as I ride in shame round this blood-stained town.
And when the poem refuses to believe
and slimes to aloes in my hands
mine is the task of burying the dead
I the late madonna of barren lands.

Garden of the Women Once Fallen

I
SHAME MI LADY

Lady, what could you have done so
to make you close in on yourself so?

The lady folds her arms across her chest.
The lady droops her head between her breasts.

The lady's eyes will not answer yours.
Lady, if I tell you my crime
will you tell me yours?

Mine are legion and all to do with love misplaced
yet I've been replanted in this arboreal place.
Now, if I can find favor (me with my bold face)
you bashful you shy you innocent lady
must/bound to find absolution/grace.

Come lady, tie bright ribbon-grass round your waist.
Let you and I bloom redemption in this place.

II
BROOM WEED

You exhaust yourself so
O weed powerless
your life devoted to sweeping, cleaning
even in your fullest blooming.

12

You pull dust balls from the air
whisk away bee-droppings
with your coarsened hair.
And in your fullness
they bundle you
without so much
as a by-your-leave.
Drudges, make a coat of arms
wear broomweed on your sleeves.

III
POUI

She don't put out for just anyone.
She waits for HIM
and in his high august heat
he takes her
and their celestial mating
is so intense
that for weeks her rose-gold dress
lies tangled round her feet
and she don't even notice.

IV
SUNFLOWER POSSESSED

Her folded neck-skin
reveals her age
but the face powdered
is limned by myriads
of mirrors and gold-washed frills.
This display is for the benefit
of the perfect one in the sky.
To the ragged coterie of weeds round her
she says, 'In my first bloom I was
the tender honey-skinned mamma
of that great golden one on high.'
The ragged weeds
never knowing glory
(for this reason some weeds are evil)
shiver their rags and hiss

'sure'
she semaphores, hoping
the golden circle of her unmaking
will give her the go-round once more.

Songs for My Son

I

My son cries
the cats answer
I hover over his sleeping
suspended on his milk-stained breath
I live in fear of his hurt, his death.
The fear is real.
If I close my eyes when it is at its height
I see him curled man-in-miniature asleep.
I hover over his milk-stained breath
and listen for its rise
every one an assurance that he is alive
and if God bargains
I strike a deal with him,
for his life I owe you something, anything,
but please let no harm come to him.
The cat cries
my son answers
his sleep is short
his stomach hurts.

II

They gather from beyond
through the trees they come
gather on the banks of the family river
one by one they raise the keening song
great grandmother Rebecca of the healing hands
Tata Edward, Bucky, and Brownman

my father's lost mother Maria
and now my father
come to sing the birthsong
and Hannah horsewoman to ride me through.
It's a son, a great grand grandson, a man
born to a headstrong, heartfoolish woman,
past the birth waters with river-washed hands
and let the newson through,
woman born of strong-limbed woman
woman born to parents in peacetime
behold your son
flesh of your flesh
your life's work begun.

III

The midwife
tie-head African woman
fingers like healing-roots
feeds me thyme-tea
to hurry on your coming
summons the appropriate spirits
to witness your crowning,
a knife keen with garlic
to sever you from me
and we'll never smell
its primal top-notes
you or I
without memories of our joining.

IV

I'll name you Miles I say
for the music, and for coming
a long way
you suck, my womb pulls
the thirst constant
the connection three-way.

My Will

Son, my will,
albeit premature
when the palm readers
divine
for me an extended
life line.

Besides who knows what
worth bequeathing
I could acquire
before the life line
inches to the darker side
of my hand.

But, for a start,
the gift of song,
this sweet immediate source
of release was not given me
so I leave it for you in the hope
that God takes hints.

Then the right to call
all older than you
Miss, mister, or mistress
in the layered love of our
simplest ways,
eat each day's salt and bread
with praise,
and may you never know hungry.
And books,
I mean the love of them.

May you like me earn good
friends
but just to be sure,
love books.
When bindings fall apart
they can be fixed
you will find
that is not always so

with friendships.

And no gold.
Too many die/kill for it
besides its face is too bold.
This observation is the
last I give:
most times assume
a patina a shade subdued
so when you bloom they
will value it.

Caravanserai

Elliptical moon
rims the yellow/brown
woman
dream seller.
Brass basins of blood
brass basins of wine
a pebbled hourglass
to texture time.

She dyes her palms
and divines on sand.
The moon bellied-out
stirs the tides' motion
within
the infant heads down
for the beginning.
The tide water breaks
the motion stays her hand.

And did you see
that quiet caravan
with muffled bells
and no colors to speak of
except the face

ebony/indigo
of the young camel driver
dream buyer?

He spoke to her of nights
by the Nile,
said there was Egypt
in her hair
and watered down
at the caravanserai there.

The Mulatta as Penelope

Tonight I'll pull your limbs through small
soft garments
your head will part my breasts
and you will hear a different heartbeat.
Today we said the real good-bye, he and I
but this time
I will not sit and spin and spin
the door open to let the madness in
till the sailor finally weary
of the sea
returns with tin souvenirs and a claim
to me.
True, I returned from the quayside
my eyes full of sand
and his salt leaving smell
fresh on my hands.
But you're my anchor awhile now
and that goes deep,
I'll sit in the sun and dry my hair
while you sleep.

'Mine, O Thou Lord of Life,
Send My Roots Rain'
– Gerard Manley Hopkins

For I've been planted long
in a sere dry place
watered only occasionally
with odd overflows
from a passing cloud's face.
In my morning
I imitated the bougainvillea
(in appearances
I'm hybrid)
I gave forth defiant alleluias
of flowering
covered my aridity with
red-petaled blisters
grouped close, from far
they were a borealis of
save-face flowers.
In the middle of my
life span
my trunk's not so limber
and sap flows thicker
my region has posted signs
that speak of scarce water.
At night God, I feel
my feet powder.
Lord let the preying worms
wait to feast in vain.
In this noon of my orchard
send me deep rain.

Keith Jarrett – Rainmaker

Piano man
my roots are African
I dwell in the center of the sun.
I am used to its warmth
I am used to its heat
I am seared by its vengeance
(it has a vengeful streak)

So my prayers are usually
for rain.
My people are farmers
and artists
and sometimes the lines
blur
so a painting becomes a
december of sorrel
a carving heaps like a yam hill
or a song of redemption wings
like the petals of resurrection
lilies – all these require rain.
So this sunday
when my walk misses
my son's balance on my hips
I'll be alright if you pull down
for me
waterfalls of rain.
I never thought a piano
could divine
but I'm hearing you this morning
and right on time
it's drizzling now
I'll open the curtains and
watch the lightning conduct
your hands.

Invoke Mercy Extraordinary
for Angels Fallen

In his 30th year
in search of signs
God's face appeared to him
on the surface of a brackish pond
littered with leaves.
The face of God
was so suffused with light
light so intense
that the rotting leaves
were cremated
and the salt-sullen water
rose clear.

Thereafter he would say,
The face of God
cannot be described
but I am grateful
I was kneeling.
And the man kneeling
and the man kneeling
heard in his head
a mighty keening.

Who knows what God
in his speaking
said to the man kneeling
but messages lodged in his lungs
were released
as a clean new source of singing.

What else is there
for the eyes to hold in wonder
after they have framed
the face of God?
He spent a lifetime after
alchemizing the visage
from pain and white powder.

Invoke mercy extraordinary
for angels fallen.
Father,
hasten the end.

Lullaby for Jean Rhys

SLEEP IT OFF LADY
the night nurse is here,
dressed in rain forest colors,
used stars in her hair.
Drink this final dark potion
and straighten your night-dress,
wear your transparent slippers
you must look your best.
For you just might go dancing
atop hard-headed trees
with a man who is virile
and anxious to please.

Sleep now Miss Rhys.

I Am Becoming My Mother

Yellow/brown woman
fingers smelling always of onions

My mother raises rare blooms
and waters them with tea
her birth waters sang like rivers
my mother is now me

My mother had a linen dress
the color of the sky
and stored lace and damask
tablecloths
to pull shame out of her eye.

I am becoming my mother
brown/yellow woman
fingers smelling always of onions.

Guinea Woman

Great grandmother
was a guinea woman
wide eyes turning
the corners of her face
could see behind her,
her cheeks dusted with
a fine rash of jet-bead warts
that itched when the rain set up.

Great grandmother's waistline
the span of a headman's hand,
slender and tall like a cane stalk
with a guinea woman's antelope-quick walk
and when she paused,
her gaze would look to sea
her profile fine like some obverse impression
on a guinea coin from royal memory.

It seems her fate was anchored
in the unfathomable sea
for great grandmother caught the eye of a sailor
whose ship sailed without him from Lucea harbor.
Great grandmother's royal scent of
cinnamon and scallions
drew the sailor up the straits of Africa,
the evidence my blue-eyed grandmother
the first Mulatta,
taken into backra's household
and covered with his name.

They forbade great grandmother's
guinea woman presence.
They washed away her scent of
cinnamon and scallions,

23

controlled the child's antelope walk,
and called her uprisings rebellions.

But, great grandmother,
I see your features blood dark
appearing
in the children of each new
breeding.
The high yellow brown
is darkening down.
Listen, children,
it's great grandmother's turn.

Nanny

My womb was sealed
with the molten wax
of killer bees
for nothing should enter
nothing should leave
the state of perpetual siege
the condition of the warrior.

From then my whole body would quicken
at the birth of every one of my people's children.
I was schooled in the green-giving ways
of the roots and vines
made accomplice to the healing acts
of Chainey root, fever grass & vervain.

My breasts flattened
settled unmoving against my chest
my movements ran equal
to the rhythms of the forest.

I could sense and sift
the footfall of men
from the animals

24

and smell danger
death's odor
in the wind's shift.

When my eyes rendered
light from the dark
my battle song opened
into a solitaire's moan
I became most knowing
and forever alone.

And when my training was over
they circled my waist with pumpkin seeds
and dried okra, a traveler's jigida,
and sold me to the traders
all my weapons within me.
I was sent, tell that to history.

When your sorrow obscures the skies
other women like me will rise.

For My Mother
(May I Inherit Half Her Strength)

My mother loved my father
I write this as an absolute
in this my thirtieth year
the year to discard absolutes

he appeared, her fate disguised,
as a sunday player in a cricket match,
he had ridden from a country
one hundred miles south of hers.

She tells me he dressed the part,
visiting dandy, maroon blazer,
cream serge pants, seam like razor
and the beret and the two-tone shoes.

My father stopped to speak to her sister,
till he looked and saw her by the oleander,
sure in the kingdom of my blue-eyed grandmother.
He never played the cricket match that day.

He wooed her with words and he won her.
He had nothing but words to woo her,
on a visit to distant Kingston he wrote,

'I stood on the corner of King Street and looked,
and not one woman in that town was lovely as you.'

My mother was a child of the petite bourgeoisie
studying to be a teacher, she oiled her hands
to hold pens.

My father barely knew his father, his mother died young,
he was a boy who grew with his granny.

My mother's trousseau came by steamer through the snows of
        Montreal
where her sisters Albertha of the cheekbones and the
perennial Rose, combed Jewlit backstreets with French-
turned names for Doris's wedding things.

Such a wedding Harvey River, Hanover, had never seen.
Who anywhere had seen a veil fifteen chantilly yards long?
and a crêpe de chine dress with inlets of silk godettes
and a neck-line clasped with jeweled pins?

And on her wedding day she wept. For it was a brazen bride in
        those days who smiled,
and her bouquet looked for all the world like a sheaf of wheat
against the unknown of her belly,
a sheaf of wheat backed by maidenhair fern, representing Harvey
        River
her face washed by something other than river water.

My father made one assertive move, he took the imported cherub
        down
from the heights of the cake and dropped it in the soft territory
between her breasts . . . and she cried.

When I came to know my mother many years later, I knew her as
    the figure
who sat at the first thing I learned to read: 'SINGER', and she
    breast-fed
my brother while she sewed; and she taught us to read while she
    sewed and
she sat in judgment over all our disputes as she sewed.

She could work miracles, she would make a garment from a
    square
in a span that defied time. Or feed twenty people on a stew made
    of
fallen-from-the-head cabbage leaves and a carrot and a cho-cho
    and a palm full of meat.

And she rose early and sent us clean into the world and she
    went to bed
in the dark, for my father came in always last.

There is a place somewhere where my mother never took the
    younger ones
a country where my father with the always smile
my father whom all women loved, who had the perpetual quality
given only to a child . . . hurt his bride.

Even at his death there was this 'Friend' who stood by her side,
but my mother is adamant that that has no place in the memory
    of my father.

When he died, she sewed dark dresses for the women amongst
    us
and she summoned that walk, straight-backed, that she gave to
    us
and buried him dry-eyed.

Just that morning, weeks after,
she stood delivering bananas from their skin
singing in that flat hill country voice

she fell down a note to the realization that she did
not have to be brave, just this once,
and she cried.

For her hands grown coarse with raising nine children
for her body for twenty years permanently fat
for the time she pawned her machine for my sister's
Senior Cambridge fees
and for the pain she bore with the eyes of a queen

and she cried also because she loved him.

Letters to the Egyptian

1

In case you do not recognize me
when I arrive at Alexandria
I will be wearing a long loose
jade green dress
my hair will be hidden
under a striped fringed headscarf
and I will smell of roseapples and musk.
O love, forgive my vanity,
it is also to make sure
you recognize me
five pounds lighter
drawn from the long journey.
I will bring you a garland
of search-mi-heart leaves.
On their underside
I've sewn some woman's tongue seeds.
You said you loved my chatter.

2

When the longboat
drew into Khartoum
where the White Nile meets the Blue
I was tempted to abandon ship.
You see there was this Kushite once

who . . .
But how could he ever
compare to you?
I settled instead for buying
at a bazaar Sheba's silver earrings
facsimiles of tiny steeds they are
sprouting forged feathered wings.
For you I found a brass horse
one hand high
you can ride across a table's distance,
some sweet salve for easing knots
in shoulders
and a purchase now private
till we're alone and unveil it.
O how could I have thought of
the Kushite –
And am I now nearer to you?
Does the Nile hold all the world's water?
How far is Khartoum from you?

3

Last night there was such
a storm at sea
I sought level
and chained myself with prayers.
(They held)
and in the after
in the soughing of the wind
I'm sure it was you
I heard sing.
Sleep now beloved
fold yourself in softened sails
I wait for you in the Aftergale.
Calm will be our mooring.

'I Shall Light a Candle of Understanding
in Thine Heart Which Shall Not Be Put Out'
– Esdras

I shall light.
First debts to pay and fences to mend,
lay to rest the wounded past, foes disguised as friends.

I shall light a candle

Cease the training of impossible hedges round this life
for as fast as you sow them, serendipity's thickets will appear
and outgrow them.

I shall light a candle of understanding in thine heart.

All things in their place then, in this many-chambered heart.
For each thing a place and for HIM a place apart.

I shall light a candle of understanding in thine heart
which shall not be put out.

By the hand that lit the candle.
By the never to be extinguished flame.
By the candle-wax which wind-worried drips
into candle wings luminous and rare.
By the illumination of that candle
exit, death and fear and doubt,
here love and possibility
within a lit heart, shining out.

This Is a Hymn
For Michael Granzen

For all who ride the trains
all night
sleep on sidewalks and park benches
beneath basements
and abandoned buildings
this is a hymn.

For those whose homes
are the great outdoors
the streets their one big room
for live men asleep in tombs
this is a hymn.

This is a hymn for bag women
pushing rubbish babies
in ridiculous prams
dividing open lots
into elaborate architects' plans.

Mansions of the dispossessed
magnificence of desperate rooms
kings and queens of homelessness
die with empty bottles
rising from their tombs.

This is a hymn
for all recommending
a bootstrap as a way
to rise with effort
on your part.
This is a hymn
may it renew
what passes for your heart.

This hymn
is for the must-be-blessed
the victims of the world
who know salt best

the world tribe
of the dispossessed
outside the halls of plenty
looking in
this is a benediction
this is a hymn.

Heartease I

We with the straight eyes
and no talent for cartography
always asking
'How far is it to Heartease?'
and they say,
'Just around the corner.'

But that being the spider's direction
means each day finds us further away.
Dem stick wi up
dem jook wi down
and when dem no find
what dem com fi find
them blood we and say
'walk wid more next time.'

So, take up divining again
and go inna interpretation
and believe the flat truth
left to dry on our tongues.
Truth say,
Heartease distance
cannot hold in a measure
it say
travel light
you are the treasure.
It say
you can read map

even if you born
a Jubilee
and grow with your granny
and eat crackers for your tea.
It say
you can get license
to navigate
from sail board horse
in the sea's gully.

Believe, believe
and believe this
the eye know how far
Heartease is.

Heartease II

In what looked like the blackout last week
a meteorite burst from the breast of the sky
smoking like a censer, it spelled out in
incandescent calligraphy
a message for all who had deep eyes.

If you did not see it I'll tell you what
it said:
Cultivate the search-mi-heart and
acres of sincerity grass and turn your
face towards Heartease.

Set out a wash pan and catch mercy rain
forget bout drought, catch the mercy rain,
bathe and catch a light from this meteoric flame
and sit down cleansed, to tell a rosary of your
ancestor's names,
a singing chain of ancient names to bind them tight
all who work evil downward through the night.

And toward morning the sun come and tell you
'sleep, I'll mark your place with this azure/rose ribbon
taken from the hidden locks of the dawn,
sleep in the day and you will dream when you sleep
the second surah of this message.'

And who hear, do all that and sleep in the darkened day and
dream as them sleep, how the one whose hand draw the veil,
(for it was not a blackout) the one who fling the meteor
was in a celestial vexation
saying, Imagine, how I put you here so in this most favored place
and look how you take it and less count it.
Look how you root up my rarest blooms,
look how you take my flower bed dem turn tombs,
look how you eye red from looking over a next one yard
from envying everything him have.
Like him concrete-stressed-cast-iron-lawn
and him man-made-robot-made-by-man-to-replace-man,
you want to know how far this thing gone?
Some calling Siberia a nice open land.
At this point it look like him was too grieved to go on
him had to drink some dew water from the throat
of a glass-petaled flower.
And when his wrath was dampened he spoke again:

I have many names and one is merciful . . .
So in that name I have decided that the veil I draw
will be lifted when you look to the condition of
your part of this yard.
When you stop draw blood cross the promise line in the
young people's palms.
When the scribes cleanse their hands and rise to write
new psalms.
When you sight up why outta the whole human race
is you of all people I choose to dwell in this place.
So who hear send me here to tell you say
we do not know bout the intentions of a next one
but we catch mercy rain in zinc and tub pan
and in addition
to the search-mi-heart
the sincerity seeds
and the pilgrimage to Heartease

34

we planting some one-love
undivided ever-living healing trees
and next week if you want to come, welcome
for we going to set up again
to extend the singing rosary of our ancestors' names
till the veil is rent from

of everyone
forever and ever
illumination.

Heartease III

In this year of cataclysm pre-predicted
being plagued with dreams
of barefoot men marching
and tall civilizations crumbling
forward to where the gathering, gathering.
Crowdapeople, crowdapeople weep and mourn,
crowdapeople I have seen
packed in Japanese carriers
dark corpses of fallen warriors.
A man wearing a dub image of dirt
roots for fodder in a garbage can
raises a filth-encrusted hand
in a dumb acceptance/greeting
of the stasis on the land.
You see it crowdapeople?

Look and marvel
for I have seen the wonder
of the candyman's posse
women laden like caravels with gold
trimmed in fur, booted in leather
crowned in picture hats
skeeled O Panama.

O wear all this together
in the height of 98-degree weather.
Be acquainted with things to come,
behold the force transparent
mirror the cynical face of the crowd.
Lead them down to dungeons of slackness
everybody follow.
Soak them in the river of darkness
everybody wallow.

Crowdapeople, crowdapeople.
Big Massa knows
that them powder the devil
and sell you
fi draw him up yu nose.
Crowdapeople,
settle.
Crowdapeople,
level.
When you gone so wide
you will encounter
your true selves again
from the starting-over side.

Then . . .
Say of the waters of the Hope river
how much sweeter than the ferment wine,
say of the simple leavened loaf
'you are the wafer.'
Accept this healing unbeliever
place truth on your tongue deceiver.
Gather, for the days wrongly predicted
by short-tongued ones will end,
these days are but a confused overture to the real
movement, to the pulsing of the rhythms
of the first and last grouping,
we will rise triumphant, clean singing.
For the righteous planted in this place
have access unlimited to the gardens of grace.
I speak no judgment
this voice is to heal
to speak of possibility

for in dreams Big Massa show me
say,
'I know my people, I created them
their ways are strange only to who will
not love and accept them,
what they do best is to be.'
No judgment I speak
that function is not mine
I come only to apply words
to a sore and confused time.

So . . .
If we mix a solution
from some wild bees' honey
and some seach-mi-heart extract
better than red conscience money
and we boil it in a bun-pan
over a sweet wood fire
make the soft smell of healing
melt hard hearts and bare wire.
If we take it and share it
so everyone get a taste
and it reach till
it purge evil from this place
till we start again clean
from the birthplace
of the stream,
while above us arches
the mercy span
a high onyx beam;
reaching from the sea
to the cobalt
blue mountain ridge
the azure forgiving
of the wide mercy bridge.

And . . .
Suppose we call out the
singers and musicians
by their hidden holy names
and then pull out from the belly
bottom of the drum and the bass

chords that quake evil and
make holy spirit raise,
while the rest of we planting the
undivided, ever-living
healing trees,
what a glory
possibility
soon come
HEARTEASE . . .

Heartease New England 1987

I see a bird trapped
under the iron girders of the Ashmont station overpass.
It is trying to measure the distance between columns
with its given wing span, and it fails
for being alone and not having a wing span wide enough.
I am told that birds travel faster over greater distances
when they move in chevron formation
a group of birds could measure the width of the Ashmont
station overpass . . . I know how the bird feels.
I have come to see the backyards of the richest lands
on earth, their basements, their backrooms,
I have seen the poor asleep in carcasses of rooms.
Those who sleep together are fortunate
not to be one of the ultimate dispossessed
the truly homeless are usually alone
and tend to wakefulness.
In the fall I search for signs
a pattern in the New England flaming trees
'What is my mission? Speak, leaves'
(for all journeys have hidden missions).
The trees before dying, only flame brighter
maybe that is the answer, live glowing while you can.

That is the only answer, except one evening in November
I see an African in Harvard Square.
He is telling himself a story as he walks

in telling it, he takes all the parts
and I see that he has taken himself home.
And I have stories too, until I tell them
I will not find release, that is my mission.
Some nights though, anxiety assails me
a shroud spinning in the snow.
They say it's the affliction of this age,
it appears unasked, an unwelcome companion
who always wants you
to sit down and die with him
when for your own good you should keep going.
I know how the bird trying to measure the overpass feels.
I too can never quite get the measure of this world's structure
somewhere I belong to community, there
I am part of a grouping of many souls and galaxies
I am part of something ever evolving, familiar, and most mighty
I reaffirm this knowing one evening, a Wednesday
as I go up Shephard Street. Someone is playing
Bob Marley and the notes are levitating
across the Garden Street end of the street.
They appear first as notes and then feather into birds
pointing their wings, arranging themselves for traveling
long distances.
And birds are the soul's symbol, so I see
that I am only a sojourner here but I came as friend
came to record and sing and then, depart.
For my mission this last life is certainly this
to be the sojourner poet caroling for peace
calling lost souls to the way of Heartease.

*The Woman Speaks to the Man
Who has Employed Her Son*

Her son was first made known to her
as a sense of unease, a need to cry
for little reasons and a metallic tide
rising in her mouth each morning.

Such signs made her know
that she was not alone in her body.
She carried him full term
tight up under her heart.

She carried him like the poor
carry hope, hope you get a break
or a visa, hope one child go through
and remember you. He had no father.
The man she made him with had more
like him, he was fair-minded
he treated all his children
with equal and unbiased indifference.

She raised him twice, once as mother
then as father, set no ceiling
on what he could be doctor,
earth healer, pilot take wings.
But now he tells her he is working
for you, that you value him so much
you give him one whole submachine gun
for him alone.

He says you are like a father to him
she is wondering what kind of father
would give a son hot and exploding
death, when he asks him for bread.
She went downtown and bought three
and one-third yards of black cloth
and a deep crowned and veiled hat
for the day he draws his bloody salary.

She has no power over you and this
at the level of earth, what she has
are prayers and a mother's tears
and at knee city she uses them.
She says psalms for him
she reads psalms for you
she weeps for his soul
her eyewater covers you.

She is throwing a partner
with Judas Iscariot's mother
the thief on the left-hand side
of the cross, his mother
is the banker, her draw though
is first and last for she is still
throwing two hands as mother and father.
She is prepared, she is done. Absalom.

Recommendation for Amber

With her, you would have a guide
to the small nubians in the garden.
They live only under bushes
that have never known knives.

They come out at night
riding on seasonal cicadas
whose noise is a radar guide,
they have given her minute boxes

of see-in eye ointment.
A very little rubbed on the eyes
makes you see good duppies.
With her Mondays could be Sundays

She would go to church on Monday
then stay indoors all afternoon
sleeping, because there is no
difference in days with Amber.

No matter how she tries she loses
things (she is not orderly).
But she will summon them back again
by invoking their names over and over.

So if you pass outside her window
and hear her repeating insistently
'keys' or 'comb', just know
that this is her strange ceremony,

the finding of lost objects.
Invariably she finds what's missing
or if it's taken, in its place will come
something amazingly much better.

She is blessed with a remarkable nose,
she can identify the ingredients
in perfumes just so, like she can
isolate the trail of the gentler tuberose

from beneath the more sensual oil slick
smell of the cat glands secreting civet.
She also knows the secret properties
of gemstones. Take amber itself, her name.

Though neither rare, costly, nor a gem
but the golden night sweat of a tree
compassionate and resilient, it's special
because it is self-healing.

Despite her tendency to wearing her hair
wild and her slow Egyptian eyes which are
fixed always above her employer's head
she has a good hand at plain cooking.

On Becoming a Tiger

The day that they stole her tiger's-eye ring
was the day that she became a tiger.
She was inspired by advice received from Rilke

who recommended that, if the business of drinking
should become too bitter,
that one should change oneself into wine.

The tiger was actually always asleep
inside her, she had seen it
stretched out, drowsing and inert

when she lay upon her side and stared
for seven consecutive days into a tall mirror
that she had turned on its side.

Her focus had penetrated all exterior
till at last she could see within her
a red glowing landscape of memory and poems,

a heart within her heart
and lying there big, bright, and golden
was the tiger, wildly darkly striped.

At night she dreams that her mother
undresses her and discovers that, under
her outerwear, her bare limbs are marked

with the broad and urgent striations
of the huge and fierce cat of Asia
with the stunning golden quartz eyes.

She has taken to wearing long dresses
to cover the rounded tail coiling behind her.
She has filled her vases with tiger lilies

and replaced her domestic cat
with a smaller relative of hers, the ocelot.
At four in the morning she practices stalking

up and down the long expanse of the hall.
What are the ingredients in tiger's milk?
Do tigers ever mate for life?

Can she rewrite the story of Little Black Sambo?
Can a non-tiger take a tiger for a wife?
To these and other questions,

she is seeking urgent answers
now that she is living an openly
tigerly life.

Mother the Great Stones Got to Move

Mother, one stone is wedged across the hole in our history
and sealed with blood wax.
In this hole is our side of the story, exact figures,
headcounts, burial artifacts, documents, lists, maps
showing our way up through the stars; lockets of brass
containing all textures of hair clippings.
It is the half that has never been told, and some of us
must tell it.

Mother, there is the stone on the hearts of some women and men
something like an onyx, cabochon-cut
which hung on the wearer seeds bad dreams. Speaking for
the small dreamers of this earth, plagued with nightmares,
yearning for healing dreams
we want that stone to move.

Upon an evening like this, mother, when one year is making way
for another, in a ceremony attended by a show of silver stars,
mothers see the moon, milk-fed, herself a nursing mother
and we think of our children and the stones upon their future
and we want these stones to move.

For the year going out came in fat at first
but towards the harvest it grew lean.
And many mouth corners gathered white
and another kind of poison, powdered white

44

was brought in to replace what was green.
And death sells it with one hand
and with the other death palms a gun
then death gets death's picture
in the papers asking,
'where does all this death come from?'
Mother, stones are pillows
for the homeless sleep on concrete sheets.
Stone flavors soup, stone is now meat,
the hard-hearted giving our children
stones to eat.

Mother, the great stones over mankind got to move.
It's been ten thousand years we've been watching them now
from various points in the universe.
From the time of our birth as points of light
in the eternal coiled workings of the cosmos.
Roll away stone of poisoned powders come
to blot out the hope of our young.
Move stone of sacrificial lives we breed
to feed to tribalistic economic machines.
From across the pathway to mount morning
site of the rose quartz fountain
brimming anise and star water
bright fragrant for our children's future.
Mother these great stones got to move.

White Birds

At first, we liked to describe them
as doves,
the white pigeons who came to live
at this house.
Appearing first as a circle with wings,
then some blessing pulling the circle in,
so that its center became our house.
Now in these eaves

a benediction of bird.
Their nervous hearts
in sync enough
with our rhythms
they enter into this house.
So sometimes in the middle
of doing some woman's thing
I look up to find us
in a new painting.
House on a rock
with wooden floors
a boy and white pigeons.

Missing the Mountains

For years I called the Blue Mountains home.
I spent my days faceting poems from rockstones.
By moonshine I polished them, they flashed fire like true gems.

I was included then in all the views of the mountains.
The hand that flung me down to the plains
was powered by the wrath of hurricanes.

Now from the flat lands of Liguanea
I view the mountains with strict detachment.
I remark upon their range and harmony of blues.

Respect due to their majesty, I keep my distance.
I must now carry proof of my past existence
in the form of one blue stone mined near mountain heart.

I show too a wildness, an intensity
drawn from the mountains' energy.
This is a request to all left behind me.

Bury me up there in the high blue mountains
and I promise that this time I will return to teach the wind
how to make poetry from tossed about and restless leaves.

October in the Kingdom of the Poor

October, month for rainy weather.
The evening sky above thick and purple,
at its heart hidden a white and watery moon.

And I wonder, is so six o'clock stay everywhere?
Like in that place in West Africa
where I come from as a child?

Where massa come from, is so it stay too?
And one mind say I wonder too much,
wonder . . . about things that have no answer.

Sometimes when I am standing, wondering
under an October sky, purple
like the royal robes of King Solomon,

a taffeta rain-streaked lavender-purple sky
like the wide skirts of queen elizabeth's dress,
sprinkled with stars silver and spaced

so that you can count them . . .
sometimes if I stand quite still,
the sky just drapes itself round my shoulders

and I stand robed, royal in the kingdom of the poor.
And then,
the stars just come and encircle my head
in a gracious diadem.

Birth Stone

The older women wise and tell Anna
first time baby mother,
'hold a stone upon your head and follow
a straight line go home.'

For like how Anna was working in the
field, grassweeder
right up till the appointed hour
that the baby was to come.

Right up till the appointed hour
when her clear heraldic water
broke free and washed her down.

Dry birth for you young mother;
the distance between the field and home
come in like the Gobi desert now.
But your first baby must born abed.

Put the woman stone on your head
and walk through no man's land
go home. When you walk, the stone
and not you yet, will bear down.

Coir

Then, the mattress was a pallet stuffed with coir
and after a rough quota of say six hundred nights
of good dreams like pumpkin and cho cho – (new life)
pretty water – (prosperity), excrement – (money), and say
114 bad dreams of wedding – (funeral), old house
missing teeth – (death), or cats – (enemy)
the coir would feel it had taken enough pressure
and would send out vengeful needles
to bore cruelly into the skin.

Rassy our mattress man was a 'beardman' who bore
a resemblance to the monk Rasputin.
He favored garments in the color of dusk
and if his head was bent over and the light was sloping
toward evening, you could imagine him in a monk's cell,
telling beads against the next phase of his life
which would find him in control of a Tzarina.
He had one eye walled off to the public
but I could see through that curtain
the worship hidden there for my mother.

But of what use were such feelings?
He was content to receive a meal at noon from her hands
and tremble gratefully at the thought of her pointed fingers
peeling moon-white Lucea yams and seasoning meat
so that you smelled her hand;
that is, a benediction of spices would rise up
to cover you when you entered through her gates.
His movements are slow,
dark molasses is his infrequent speech.
He can sit still for what seems to a fidgety child
like 999 hours.

But something stirs his slow self into speeded up action
when Rassy whips the coir.
First he folds his handkerchief into half, three points,
a triangle, a mask. He ties it round the lower half of his face,
pulls down his cap to just above his eyes.
Then he runs his thumb and forefinger
along the thick wire of his whip.
The handle too is of wire but padded with cloth over and over.
Ready, he approaches the small red mountain, muttering
some ancient incantation to protect him from fierce fiber.
His arm jerks back and flicks forward, he delivers the first
blow, the coir registers receival of whipping
by sending out a cloud of frightened red dust.
When Rassy whips the rebellious coir he whips
all his enemies, exorcizes life pain and causes rain
to fall down red from what he sends up to the heavens.

The woman who threw the acid that coagulated his eye
first rain of blows.

49

Then the colonial Government, the Governor and Queen Victoria
for sending that heartless facety letter commending
ex-slaves to 'industry, thrift, and obedience'
when the people were just rightly asking for justice,
and land to live on and grow food.
The first man who had the idea to leave and go
to Africa and interfere with the people who were minding
their own business, a hard rain of blows.
For Mussolini and the Italian Army
on behalf of Haile Selassie, five straight minutes of blows.
To Babylon in general for generic evil, hunger, disease
bad minded people, Rassy rains blows.
He whips them all for a good part of the morning
red clouds about his head flying frightened vapor from his whip.
And when the coir has been beaten into submission
he walks away triumphant, sweating, removes the mask
and wipes his eyes, it comes away red but his blood
is running free.

He asks of my mother a cool drink
of water which he sips with the air of a victorious warrior
before he settles at the machine to stitch
the big square of new striped ticking
into which he will imprison the chastened coir.

Elephant

Memory claims that in a jungle once
a great mother elephant, crazed
with grief for her lost son,
wrapped her trunk around a baobab tree
and wrenched it free from its upside down
hold in the earth and trumpeted down
the hole in the earth for her vanished one.

Elephant, the lost the cursed one lumbers
up from under the big trees in Queen Victoria's park.
This man more pachyderm than man, skin draped loose,
grey, muddy as tarpaulin, over swollen elephantiasis limbs.
He moves bent over, weighed by the bag of crosses
over his shoulder, his lips droop tubular.
Small children appear and chant, 'elephant, elephant . . .'

He rears back on his huge hind legs trumpeting
threats of illegal surgery by broken glass bottle,
death to small children, who scatter before him like antelopes
and elands, skittering across the asphalt heading home.
Elephant, loneliest one in all creation, your friends
the night grazing mules, tethered by dark hills of coal
in Mullings grass yard.

Poor Elephant always walking
hoping one day he would turn a corner and come upon
a clearing familiar to long memory,
wide green space and baobab trees.
For there his mother and the great herds would be, free.

Bag-a-Wire

Sir, if you see Bag-a-wire walking
into the furnace of the sun at evening
can you please direct him down to Race Course?

For there he will find Marcus Garvey
the only man possessing appropriate pardon
to free him from his long and living death.

Man, if you are the one to direct him,
make sure you tell him loudly, for all his senses
are now concentrated into a laserlike stare.

A stare he trains up and down the frame
of every passing man, black, heavy-set
inclining to be pompous but majestic, giant

of a far sighted man and prophet who could be
Marcus Garvey. Prophets speak light and this one
has the luminous oratory which, dissolving dark,

could finally set Bag-a-wire free.
For when he sees him finally (a scene he has played
in his mind often) he will kneel so contrite:

on the government sidewalk a fallen knight kneels
and puts his forehead to the shoe of the visionary
whom he sold for food, saying 'Sir, I beg your pardon

I am related by hard design and infamy
to a line of betrayers without whom saviors
can never fulfil their shining destiny . . .'

Bun Down Cross Roads

Bun Down Cross Roads, ex-esquire, former gentleman
of substance and shopkeeper.
Now convicted arsonist and fruit seller.
Special purveyor of heavy-jowled governor mango
and scowling coarse skinned ugli fruit.

Bun Down could concoct in ripe and fruity tones
unique and extravagant combinations
of forty shilling words and never repeat
a particular formation once, in the distance
between King Street and Cross Roads.

Legend of Bun Down, bad word merchant, goes
he is arrested, brought before her majesty's court
for using decent language, indecently.

Bun Down is fined for one forty shilling word.
And in a gesture befitting his better days,

thrust his hand deep down into the pocket
of his rusty black serge suit and extracts
a crisp and freshly inked ten pound note.
It crackles in the courtroom air and Bun Down
rolls his baritone providing rich timbre, under.

'I have on my person these ten pounds, I wish
to curse until I have reached this sum.'

And so said, so it was done.

In City Gardens Grow No Roses as We Know Them

Outside the street ran hard
a still dark river of asphalt.
At the core of the many-celled tenement
lay the central brick-paved courtyard
severe square of unyielding red soil
for the only tree in one hundred and seventeen
Orange Street.

The long blunted silver trunk
of a decapitated breadfruit tree
beheaded by a blind flying sheet
of zinc driven by a hurricane's fury.
Still the tree refused to die completely
but stood leaning forward to the East
as if hoping to receive something regenerative.

A thick crown of new leaves/antlers of branches,
blossoms that bud into brown swords
fruit like green globes, scale-backed dripping staining sap
tasting like fresh baked bread after

its white dense flesh has passed through fire.
The only tree, half alive in 117 Orange Street
standing headless defiant and hoping.

Awaiting a last fruitfulness, a new life and greening
paying obeisance at the site of the sun's religious rising.
And the people planted what they could.
In paved yards with no lawns they planted.
In discarded paint pans that they filled
with fertile soil they transported in bags
from the green growing yards of St Andrew.

In St Andrew's houses they worked as maids
as nurses to small children calling big women
by their first names. Big women who called children
miss or mister, or young missis or young massa.
They worked as yard boys even when
they were shuffling work worn old men.

They were cooks in the kitchens of gracious homes
who cooked their meals outside on coal pot stoves.
The second cooking after the big house dinner
was the twilight cooking of provender
rank salted fish and offal, tuberous ground provisions,
the food of slavery, unfit for high tables.
Food that smelled like sweat and strong seasoning

with the musk fragrance of coconut oil pervading
the dusk outside the big house, they ate
from enamel or tin plates, cheap utensils set aside
for the exclusive use of yardboys and maids.
Bent forks dull knives of base metal
and for the belly-wash, sangaree of poor people,
a tin can with a soldered on kimbo of a handle.

Sometimes though like Lazarus they got what was left
from the tables of the people with plenty.
They carried it home in bags, the good earth
like loose dark fruitcake, alluvial gold,
rich soil from the yards of plenty
for the paint pan gardens in the paved yards
of the poor who lived in the city.

They planted mint first, spiked lancelike leaves
of black mint, fragrant light green peppermint.
Mint tea, necessary for the soothing of stomachs,
cure all to bad feeling and nonspecific discomforts.
Mint for the benediction its leaves exuded
when the early morning breezes moved away
from the side of the sea and passed through dense places.

Breezes like kind overseers or benign landlords
or land missus inspecting rented places.
Maybe they planted mint as a green barometer
for that is how you would know if angels passed,
when the mint plants would shudder and send out
their sweet sharp mint fragrance.
After all, everyone knows that when angels pass

through noisy crowds everyone falls suddenly silent.
Maybe then mint is the scent of angels.
Source of divine perfume with dark sharp base notes
rising up to tender green top notes
distilled to become essential oil of fresh anointing.
Planted strategically outside the welcoming doors
to measure the movement of angels.

Occasionally, an old chamber pot
would be transformed, pressed into higher service.
Battered and used, fallen into black holes
dark cavities eaten into its white enamel surface
it would become cleansed from years of low service
brought out from its shadow dwelling of nocturnal shame
and elevated to the level of respectable receptacle.

Necessary medicinal herbs, flowers easy to grow
no delicate blooms could survive here.
In city gardens grow no roses as we know them.
So the people took the name and bestowed it
generic, on all flowers, called them roses.
So here we speak a litany of the roses that grow
in the paint-pan chamber-pot gardens of Kingston.

See the quick growing four-o'-clock
that sleeps all days and springs suddenly up

55

in the afternoon, comes wide awake as if
it is the emblem of factory workers
pulling a round of the night shift.

Bright carmine pucker of bachelor buttons
for wild men who will not marry.

Dangling furry fall of puss tail,
Sansivira or Donkey's ears,
the tuneful Monkey fiddle.
Perfect plants for yards where tyrannical landlords
allow no animals.

And all gardens then contained the necessary
the precious and bitter carminative cactus plant
flower of the aloe and the tuna.
For the restoration of lost shining.
It coats the insides and the hair and skin
with a healing shine that by some botanical alchemy
leaves behind a kind of glow.
The afterglow of the aloes experience
is a kind of halo.

The croton with its varicolored self
prefiguring abstract paintings
creating wild eccentric patterns
in multiple and riotous colors.

And the Coleus. Say its name
with reverence devout.
Say it in the ordinary tongue
call it Joseph's coat
after the splendid garment
bestowed on the dreamer
by his father.

And Joseph must be the patron saint
of poets of the city
survivors of stabbings, murder, and treachery
compelled always to interpret the dreams
the visions of lovers, paupers, beggars, kings.

Renewed, renewed by the angel smell of mint.
Lulled to sleep by the running stream of traffic,
walking by the dark asphalt river,
divining images from hard unyielding surfaces.

Witnessing, witnessing in crowded places.
Praying in spite of, nonetheless.
In hanging gardens in paint cans
in Babylon.

Losing their heads and praying for new life.

Weaving the patched coats of Joseph.

Fabulous lost and found again
unfraying at the selvages.

In the face of terrors, witnessing
through plagues, wars, and imprisonings.

In tenements and walled places
marking how blood spilled leaves shadows.

And the smell of fear is a harsh perfume
city dwellers wear and are used to.

But the poet offspring of Joseph
have no choice but to sing.

To dream and interpret
reminding the righteous
of the blessing active in angels' wings
which releases the smell of mint.

And leaves behind the unseen
mark upon your door.

After angels assigned to city dwellers
have come and gone
passed over.

Songs of the Fruits
and Sweets of Childhood

O small and squat
with thin tough skin
containing the slick flesh
of mackafat
which makes fillings
like putty between
the teeth.

Cream pink pomander
like a lady's sachet
is the genteel roseapple
scenting the breath.

Jade green lantern
light astringent
is the tart taste
of the jimbelin.

Tough skinned
brown pods
of stinking toe
you broke open hard
upon stone
to free the pungent
dry powdery musk
called by some,
locust.

A brittle sweet cup
brims
with a sweetish slime
in which
tiny grey-eyed seeds
seem to wink.

And coolie plums
and red/yellow
coat plums

for June time
and apples
O taheti.

But of all fruit
the most perfect is
the dark ocher
taste like rosewater
color like logwood honey
that is a naseberry.

The starapple
wears a thick coat
of royal purple
and at its center
sports a star
of many points.

This is a lover's fruit
because it runs
with a sweet
staining milk
and the flesh
if bitten too deep,
has been known to bind you.

Of the sweets
the sweets
now sing,
beginning with the sour
fleshed tamarind.

Which if rolled
into sugar
becomes balanced
into being
the yin and yang
of sweets.

A soft brown square
of rare delight
is a wedge

of guava cheese.
O guava cheese
make you sneeze.
Penny a cut
full yu gut?

And in singing
the lungs will fill
with the sweet dust
of corn,
pounded, parched
blended with
cane sugar
to tickle the
channels of breathing.
Inhale, sneeze
sing so
'Asham O.'

The rise
of the palette's roof
is a nice height
under which
to tuck the pink backed
paradise plum.
Its smooth
white underbelly
melting level
with the tongue.

A mint ball
is divided by thin
varicolored stripes
like the porcelain
marble of a prince.

A shaggy
grater cake
can be rich brown
if it takes
its color
from burnt sugar.

But if it holds
its coconut milk
to itself
and mixes only
with white sugar,
it becomes
what some consider
a greater cake.
It is then topped
with a show off hat
of cochineal or magenta.

A Bustamente backbone
is a stubborn mixture
of coconut
and caramelized sugar.
One side wears
a thin skin
of grease proof paper
which you peel off
before chewing.

Hard on the jawbone
it is,
tying up the teeth.

But the tie-teeth
is another kind
of sweet.
Tangled and sweet
like some things
tempting
but so tangled.

Hot pink
stretcher
like a fuchsia lipstick.

Whole peanuts
suspended
in crystallized sugar
is a wangla.

And the ring game
or join up
of pink top
candy bump
going round and round
in a ring
of the fruits and sweets
of childhood
sing.

Outside the Gates

Outside the high gates of the school
named for all the saints
gathered each day a band of good women
seeking a steady and righteous living
through purveying food to children.

These women in the service of children
after a time became like saints.
Their heads surrounded by straw halos
of golden Jippi-Jappa weave
through which the honey coloured sun streamed.

They sold fruits and sweets from wide baskets
balanced on upturned carton boxes,
and baked goods that they displayed
in small cabinets called showcases
with transparent gleaming glass windows.

The fruits were colored like edible jewels,
the sweets did not originate in anonymous factories,
each sweet had its own shape
stamped with its maker's hand,
each sweet was an original then.

All kind women, except for one
whom it is said had lost all her children.
We were warned to avoid her, to resist
her bitter wares, her wiles, her witch-way
of enticing small children to enter

their names into her dirty exercise book
of credit. For once their names were marked down
she would anxiously wait for them to falter
in their small debt repayment.
She was known to take great pleasure

in entering classrooms and pointing
with a crooked finger at the poor cringing debtor
who would then be punished severely
by a principled teacher, warning against
the terrible practice of crediting.

But the teacher's punishment
would become as nothing
compared to the humiliation
for days, of your classmates chanting
'yay, yay, you trust and don't pay.'

To be avoided too was Miss Gladys
the queen of the Ptomaine Palace,
her flat fritters laying drowsy
with sleeping overnight oil.
They slumbered in her show case unaware

that there were terrible rumors
about their function as mattresses
for prehistoric drummer roaches
and that her soft topped puddings
were concocted with disgusting ingredients.

Every child in the school denied
ever having given her patronage,
although she sold her greasy foodstuff
at those gates for many years,
standing near to the magician snowball man.

His painted cart a bright chariot
scarlet red with fiery wheels
and stippled with millions
of hundreds and thousands, varicolored
confetti dots and transparent streamers blowing.

The ice of his trade was contained and covered within
the carefully zinc-lined stomach.
He was a skilled ventriloquist
and a puppet master, with a doll through which
he spoke to you, for a copper willy-penny.

He created his own aerated water
in magical fantastic colors.
A lurid lime, a straw dye red
and the favorite of all children,
O the invisible cream soda.

To create snowballs, he would shave
the ice with a shiny metal wedge
which rasped over the frozen surface
until it had ingested
enough ice crystals to be pressed

into a round snowball which was then
drenched with cherry red or citron gold syrup.
Securely standing in round-fitted holes
the long-necked bottles of bright syrup rode
on display in the open shelves of the chariot.

Snow balls with syrup, an everyday treat.
Snowballs crowned with soapy ice cream
became 'back and front', every child's dream.
While around it all bounced amber and chocolate
striped bees in a sugary bumbling dance.

Annie Pengelly

I come to represent the case
of one Annie Pengelly,
maidservant, late of the San Fleming Estate
situated in the westerly parish of Hanover.

Hanover, where that masif
mountain range
assumes the shape of a Dolphin's head
rearing up in the blue expanse overhead
restless white clouds round it foaming.

Those at sea would look up
and behold, mirrored, a seascape in the sky.

It is this need to recreate,
to run 'gainst things, that cause
all this confusion.

The same need that made men
leave one side of the world
to journey in long, mawed ships,
to drogue millions of souls
to a world
that they call the new one
in competition with the original act
the creation of the old one.

So now you are telling me to proceed
and proceed swiftly.
Why have I come here representing Annie?

Well this is the first thing she asked me to say,
that Annie is not even her real name.
A name is the first thing we own in this world.

We lay claim to a group of sounds
which rise up and down and mark out our space
in the air around us.
We become owners of a harmony of vowels and consonants
singing a specific meaning.

Her real name was given to her
at the pastoral ceremony of her outdooring.
Its outer meaning was, 'she who is precious to us'.

It had too a hidden part, a kept secret.
A meaning known only to those within
the circle of her family.

For sale Bidderman, one small girl,
one small African girl answering now
to the name of Annie.

Oh Missus my dear, when you write Lady Nugent
to tell her of your splendid birthday
of the ivory moire gown you wore
that you send clear to London for.

You can tell her how you had built for you
a pair of soft, supple leather riding boots
fashioned from your own last
by George O'Brian Wilson
late of Aberdeen
now Shoemaker and Sadler of Lucea, Hanover
late occupation,
bruk Sailor.

One pair of tortoiseshell combs,
one scrolled silver backed mirror,
one dinner party where they killed
one whole cow
with oaken casks of Madeira wine
to wash it down.

And don't forget, one small African girl,
answering now to the name of Annie.

With all that birthday show of affection
Massa never sleep with missus.
But I am not here to talk about that,
that is backra business.

I am really here just representing Annie Pengelly.

For Missus began to make Annie
sleep across her feet
come December when northers began to blow.

Northers being the chill wheeling tail end
of the winter breezes
dropping off their cold what lef' in Jamaica
to confuse the transplanted Planter.

Causing them to remember words like 'hoarfrost' and 'moors'
from a frozen vocabulary they no longer
had use for.

When this false winter breeze would
careen across canefields
Missus would make Annie lie draped,
heaped across her feet
a human blanket
nothing covering her as she gave
warmth to Missus.

So I come to say that History owes Annie
the brightest woolen blanket.
She is owed too, at least twelve years of sleep
stretched out,
free to assume the stages of sleep
flat on her back,
or profiled like the characters
in an Egyptian frieze.

Most nights though, Missus don't sleep.
And as Annie was subject to Missus will,
Annie was not to sleep as long
as Missus kept her open-eyed vigil.

Sometimes Missus sit up
sipping wine from a cut glass goblet.
Talking, talking.

Sometimes Missus dance and sing
like she was on a stage,
sad cantatrice solo
on a stage performing.

At the end of her performance
she would demand that Annie clap
clap loud and shout 'encore'.

Encouraged by this she would sing
and dance on,
her half-crazed torch song of rejection.

Sometimes Annie nod off,
Missus jook her with a pearl-tipped pin.
Sometimes Annie tumble off the chair
felled by sleep.
Missus slap her awake again.
Then in order to keep her alert, awake
she devised the paper torture.

One pile of newspapers
a sharp pair of scissors later,
Annie learned about
the cruel make-work task
that is the *cut-up*
to throw-away of old newspaper.

For if Missus could not sleep
Annie gal you don't sleep that night,
and poor Missus enslaved by love
fighting her servitude with spite.

So I say history owes Annie
thousands of nights
of sleep upon a feather bed.
Soft feathers from the breast of
a free, soaring bird,
one bright blanket,
and her name returned,
she who is precious to us.

Annie Pengelly O.
I say, History owe you.

Nayga Bikkle

Yes sir, massa was always complaining about our cooking.
Massa called it 'Coarse Cuisine'.
Somehow it downright seemed to offend him
whenever nayga cooking.

'Nayga Bikkle O', all manner of ground provision.
Sing now of the tuberous diversity of yam
from different race and country.

Firm and strong, the negro yam, smooth the snow white yam.
The subtle eating chinee yam, the powdery golden yellow yam,
the aristocrat of yam the Lucea yam. Small island yam,
St Vincent yam, miniature yam, the yampie. They even have
that nice soft yam, named for the sweetness of the woman.

What could possibly be more pleasing than a hot steaming slice
of dry powdery yam protected by a salt ting watch man
and floating in a fragrant sea of plenty coconut oil?

Ah the rich, gold-fleshed pumpkin with the secret spring within
      the belly,
pointed okra pods that slide across the tongue.
The generosity of the quick growing calalloo, verdant, season up,
and steamed down.

And these are only some of the wonders of nayga bikkle.

One day in the middle of October
month for rainy weather,
as God would have it here comes massa,
master of all him survey.

One minute he was outlined against the sky
luminous in the afternoon light
which was gold and gilding his hair and skin.
The buttons upon his jacket brass and blazing.

The metal trim upon his saddle joined in the
blazing too,

till massa was beginning to seem like him was more than man,
him was taller than a cedar tree
more lofty than Blue Mountain Peak.

When the sky suddenly frown and get dark.
And in this darkness overwhelming
massa shining was suddenly dimmed.

The rain started to pour, no advance drizzle
just a big thunder clap
and the sky opened up.
The nearest place of shelter
was my little wattle and daub hut.

I say 'good evening' when massa come in.

Massa grunt two times for an answer
then him stand there growling
by the door way,
growling to outmatch the thunder.

Well sir, to think that massa could fall so low
as to have to take up shelter in my humble abode.
But the rain was falling like it had no plan for stopping.

Now as it so happens I was eating my dinner,
and what else could a poor person like me
be dining upon except coarse cuisine?

The said cuisine, that massa finds so downright offending.
And you know as I sit there I suddenly see the smells
rise up like strong spirits out of my pot
rise up and start to worry him.

Well, I was eating my dinner,
I have manners, I share a plate for massa.

When I eat, I want to sleep!
I close my eyes and when I wake, massa was gone
so was the food in the plate.

Tell anyone that I tell you that massa eat nayga bikkle.

And you know it never kill him, for him live long
and make plenty man fret,
but till the day him dead he could never truly say
that him never eat nayga bikkle yet.

Nayga Bikkle o, the integration of rices and peas,

red peas and rice or the peas of the congo that in the course of
     their transplantation
were transformed into gungoo.

The pretty little black and white black-eyed peas.
As a matter of fact, we call all beans – peas.
It's a generic tribute to the protein filled legume

that is so much a foundation stone in the architecture of nayga
     bikkle.
All peas come together with rice joined by the ubiquitous kindness
     of coconut milk,
which gives to food a texture, like silk upon the tongue.

Ah, the wonders of the salted cod fish, making tasteful intervention
in every poor somebody's dish, fried lacelike in a fritter,
mated equally with the yellow aril of the ackee.
Such cooking claims the air, its strong seasoning
drawing mouth water in anticipation of high feasting.

Behold how good and pleasant it is to taste the food
the bounty born of the plenty of our poverty.
The nayga bikkle of this land, season strong
you smell we hand?
O the wonders of Nayga Bikkle.

Name Change: Morant Bay Uprising

After the trouble
some with the name Bogle
catch fraid like sickness
and take panic for the cure.

For it was going to be hard to survive
if identified with the hung figure
revolving in the wind
from the yard arm of the *Wolverine*.

So we took bush for it
and swallow cerasee to cleanse
deacon Paul blessed name
from blood and memory.

Or some with the help of bamboo root
bend the truth into Bogie, or Boggis,
or Buddle, or some come out of that
alphabet altogether.

Some would answer to no name on earth.
Sometimes after man see hanging
as example, preach like Paul,
your words will fall on stony ground.

From the Book of Local Miracles, Largely Unrecorded

Write this truth now
of the simple faith
of my mother's friend.

Who set a pot of water
over a candlewood fire
when she knew she had no food.

And in it placed
a stone
and by it waited.

Just as the water
began to break
over the stone

enter one neighbor
with an abundance
of coconuts and ground provisions.

Then another
fresh from slaughter
offering a portion of goat's flesh.

My mother always pauses
at this point in the retelling
of the miracle

and adds to the text
'She even got oil
from the coconuts.'

All that she needed
was salt.
And widows have that.

Prophets and widows,
self-replenishing
measures of meal,

never ending cruse of oil.
Bright angels appearing
to meet believers
at points of need

come again
when these women
call out for miracles.

Some Things You Do Not Know about Me

When I am alone like this
I drink from a saucer,
I eat naturally with my fingers
and I never wear shoes.
For seven years I drank my morning tea
from the same cup.
It was a rich brown like bitter chocolate
and stippled with tiny white dots over its round surface
except all round the rim
where my constant drinking had washed those dots away.
I think I may have swallowed them, because some nights
I feel like a trillion small punctuation
periods are swarming inside me,
waiting to attach themselves
to the ends of my unwritten lines and sentences.
But that is not the most important thing about me.
You see, what I've never told you is that I'm really a dancer.
Yes, when I'm alone when nobody is watching
you should see me dancing.
Sometimes it's my dance of joy, like when
I'm writing a poem and somehow it's working,
I'm so happy that my feet start to pump up and down
like I'm playing a big baritone pipe organ.
My hands fly to the keys and out like I'm pulling out music notes,
and my feet, my feet are dancing.
If the poem is really coming now, straight and sure,
no holding it back as it heads for its union with the page,
then I simply must take advantage and dance.
So I throw my hands up over my head
thereby releasing the poem.
And then I push the chair away
and for ten minutes or so I dance around the table.
It's a whirling kind of dance I do,
it makes my head really spin,
my particular form of dancing.
Round and round the table I go
till my wild whirling
shaves the edges off the square table,
and I'm whirling now around a round table.

I go so until I fall down,
and wherever my feet are pointed
it is there that I take the poem.
Like this one, I think now I will have to take it East,
so I will light a stick of incense
and play Bob Dylan wondering
if she might be in Tangier.
Or I just might sit quietly
and take my own self there.
All this I do before I begin the evening's cooking.
And when you come home you always find me placid, calm,
    normal.
And these are only some of the things
you do not know about me.

In the Mountains of the Moon, Uganda

In the mountains of the moon, Uganda
God wept fresh tears when God's gracious heart
conceived of what it would mean
for willing souls to make the journey of peril
back to Her/Him.

From these twin streams of compassion
the Nile was born.
And your soul has followed its course
winding, bending back upon itself
forcing you to bend too.

Who can walk to where the Nile begins or ends?
You with a will of iron and a head as hard.
For no one can convince you not to follow
to its ending
what God wept to create in the beginning.

Morning, Morning Angel Mine

Four in the morning
you turn me over
to speak into me some new knowledge.

Today's lesson is about life more abundant
and sweet singing
about why we move so
to the kumina of the Congo
'All a we a one Bungo'

Why we sing so to the Yoruba of Brazil
Gilberto, Gil, Nascimento, Jobim
riffing down the lips of a stone flower.
Wonder which notes register keener
wild woman crying or wild violins.

Mornings with you Cherubim I wake
to hear you whispering all the promises you make
when we are on the earth plane and awake.
Soft in the hours of nectar
you whisper to me of promises kept
and promises in keeping.

They fall about us like angel feathers
swept with the lightest of brooms.
Airborne now are our promises
in this lit and sanctified room.

What they cannot see
is that their reality
smokes dimly at the periphery
of us. What we are about is
liquid jewels for wine

Carnelian star apples
ruby bird cherries
celebrations in a sealed space
sacred and divine.
Their striving horns

emit dull sounds and fall
as lusterless still lives.

What we are about
is outside of imagining.
Today's lesson is about
life more abundant and
sweet singing

Golden apples and
sweet cups brimming
spirit rosemary wine

Old wine skins cast off
into the flow
of the regenerating
Rio Nuevo
upon your lips
the taste of new wine

Morning morning
Angel mine.

Bulls Bay, Lucea

Today harvest Sunday
the Parish Church is full
of formal worship.

They have brought in the sheaves
and the bounty is laid
fruitful evidence at the altar.

Ribbon-striped sugar-cane and moon-white yams
is what these parts,
my mother's country, is known for.

77

An artist among them has strung
bright bulbs of hot ripe peppers
glowing high across the Altar.

The congregation sings
from the hymnal
of the Church of England,

'We plough the fields and scatter.'

I walk past the Church
down to the seaside
immersion, deep cleansing
today is what I am after.

Here there is a mother
bathing a young baby.
She is sopping, stretching its limbs
reshaping the pliant body
in the salt water.

A child is building sand structures
testing the texture of the sand
between her fingers.

Sometimes she stops and stares
out to sea
with the liquid eyes of a dreamer.

There is a youth who just emerged
from a one-room
barely high enough to stand in

he is now sitting on the low branch
of a coco plum tree.
He is smoking something.

A woman with a bitter green
body smell
is screaming at three small children
not to venture too far into the water,

which, as if belying her warning
is calm and wears a silver sheen
and laps lovingly at the shoreline.

To an observer this is a perfect
watercolor,
'Natives bathing in a benign sea,'
and the waves speak a timeless sermon

say
that all flesh is grass

say
that the only thing which lasts
is something that the eye cannot see

say
that it can work mysteriously
in the hearts of women and men

say
that it can change the plans of them
who do not count these women and these men.

The one sopping the limbs of the baby
so that it will be strong in the joints
to take life's blows.

The youth smoking something
so that the roof of his room can touch the skies
in imitation of the mercurial rise
of his dreams.

The bitterbush woman
screaming at the children
who want to run away from that voice,
sounding strident warnings repeatedly
about shark danger lurking
beneath calm seas.

And the small dreamer
wishing that she could walk upon water

across to cities of tall solid structures,
real pepper lights
but no warm watercolor sea.

Far from Bulls Bay, Lucea
where I worship, adding my salt to the sea,
repeating after the sermon of the waves

say
All flesh is grass

say
The only thing that lasts
is the enigma of a leaven
the eye cannot see . . .

say
As I baptize myself
with these people today

say
Lord have mercy on me.

To Us, All Flowers Are Roses

Accompong is Ashanti, root, Nyamekopon.
Appropriate name, Accompong, meaning
warrior or lone one. Accompong,
home to bushmasters, bushmasters being
maroons, maroons dwell in dense places
deep mountainous well sealed
strangers unwelcome. Me No Send You No Come.

I love so the names of this place
how they spring brilliant like 'roses'
(to us all flowers are roses), engage you
in flirtation. What is their meaning? Pronunciation?
A strong young breeze that just takes

these names like blossoms and waltz
them around, turn and wheel them on the tongue.

There are angels in St Catherine somewhere.
Arawak is a post office in St Ann.
And if the Spaniards hear of this
will they come again in Caravelles
to a post office (in suits of mail)
to inquire after any remaining arawaks?
Nice people, so gentle, peaceful, and hospitable.

There is everywhere here.
There is Alps and Lapland and Berlin.
Armagh, Carrick Fergus, Malvern
Rhine and Calabar, Askenish
where freed slaves went to claim
what was left of the Africa within
staging secret woodland ceremonies.

Such ceremonies! such dancing, ai Kumina!
drum sound at Barking Lodge where we hear
a cargo of slaves landed free, because
somebody sign a paper even as they
rode as cargo shackled on the high seas.
So they landed here, were unchained, went free.
So in some places there is almost pure Africa.

Some of it is lost, though, swept away forever,
maybe at Lethe in Hanover, Lethe springs
from the Greek, a river which is the river
of Oblivion. There is Mount Peace here
and Tranquility and Content. May Pen
Dundee Pen, Bamboo Pen and for me,
Faith's Pen, therefore will I write.

There is Blackness here which is sugar land
and they say is named for the ebony of the soil.
At a wedding there once the groom wore cobalt blue
and young bride, cloud white, at Blackness.
But there is blood, red blood in the fields
of our lives, blood the bright banner flowing
over the order of cane and our history.

The Hope River in hot times goes under,
but pulses underground strong enough to rise
again and swell to new deep, when the May rains
fall for certain. There was a surfeit once
of Swine in Fat Hog quarter and somehow
Chateau Vert slipped on the Twi of our tongue
and fell to rise up again as 'Shotover'.

They hung Paul Bogle's body at sea
so there is blood too in the sea, especially
at Bloody Bay where they punctured balloons
of great grey whales. There is Egypt here
at Catadupa, a name they spoke first softly
to the white falling cataracts of the Nile.
There is Amity and Friendship and Harmony Hall.

Stonehenge . . . Sevens, Duppy Gate, Wait a Bit,
Wild Horses, Tan and See, Time and Patience,
Unity. It is Holy here, Mount Moses
dew falls upon Mount Nebo, south of Jordan,
Mount Nebo, rises here too hola Mount Zion high.
Paradise is found here, from Pisgah we look out
and Wait a Bit, Wild Horses, Tan and See,
Time and Patience, Unity.

For the wounded a Doctor's Cave
and at Phoenix Park from Burnt Ground new rising.
Good Hope, the mornings dawn crystalline
at Cape Clear. It is good for brethren
and sistren to dwell together in Unity
on Mount Pleasant. Doctor Breezes issue from the side
of the sea across parishes named for saints.

Rivers can be tied together in eights.
Mountains are Lapis Lazuli or Sapphire,
impossibly blue, and rivers wag their waters
or flow Black or White or of Milk.
And the waters of the Fish River do contain
and will yield up, good eating fish. O heart
when some nights you cannot sleep,

for wondering why you have been charged
to keep some things of which you cannot speak,
think what release will mean, when your name
is changed to Tranquility. I was born at Lineen –
Jubilee! – on the anniversary of Emancipation Day.
I recite these names in a rosary, speak them
when I pray, for Heartease, my Mecca, aye Jamaica.

After the Green Gown of My Mother Gone Down

August, her large heart slows down then stops.
Fall now, and trees flame, catch a fire and riot

last leaves in scarlet and gold fever burning.
Remember when you heard Bob Marley hymn

'Redemption Song', and from his tone and timbre
you sensed him traveling? He had sent the band home

and was just keeping himself company, cooling star,
sad rudeboy fretting on cowboy box guitar

in a studio with stray echo and wailing sound
lost singing scatting through the door of no return.

When the green goes, beloved, the secret is opened.
The breath falls still, the life covenant is broken.

Dress my mother's cold body in a deep green gown.
Catch a fire and let fall and flame time come

after the green gown of my mother gone down.

We laid her down, full of days,
chant griot from the book of life,
summon her kin from the long-

lived line of David and Margaret.
Come Cleodine, Albertha,
Flavius, Edmund, Howard and Rose,
Marcus her husband gone before
come and walk Dear Doris home.

And the Blue Mountains will open to her
to seal her corporeal self in.
From the ancient vault
that is their lapis lazuli heart
the headwaters of all our rivers spring.
Headwaters, wash away the embalmer's myrrh resin
the dredging of white powder caking her cold limbs.

Return her ripe body clean
to fallow the earth.
Her eyes to become brown agate stones.
From her forehead let there dawn
bright mornings.
May her white hair contribute
to the massing of clouds

cause the blood settled in her palms
to sink into fish-filled lagoons.
Earth, she was a mother like you
who birthed and nursed her children.
Look cherubims and angels, see her name
written down in the index of the faithful
in the mother-of-pearl book of saints.

Mama, Aunt Ann says
that she saw Aunt Rose
come out of an orchard
red with ripe fruit
and called out laughing to you.
And that you scaled the wall
like two young girls
scampering barefoot among
the lush fruit groves.

My Mother's Sea Chanty

I dream that I am washing
my mother's body in the night sea
and that she sings slow
and that she still breathes.

I see my sweet mother
a plump mermaid in my dreams
and I wash her white hair
with ambergris and foaming seaweed.

I watch my mother under water
gather the loose pearls she finds,
scrub them free from nacre
and string them on a lost fishing line.

I hear my dark mother
speaking sea-speak with pilot fish,
showing them how to direct barks
that bear away our grief and anguish.

I pray my mother breaks free
from the fish pots and marine chores
of her residence beneath the sea,
and that she rides a wild white horse.

The Domestic Science of Sunday Dinner

There is the soaking of the peas; the red kidney beans
dried out from hard life, which need to be revived
through the water process, overnight osmosis.

There is the seasoning of the meat
always with garlic which you scrape
with the serrated edge of an Okapi knife.

Mince these cloves of pungent flavor
then slice the circular onions, weeping
add the savor of salt and the bite of pepper,

add pimento kernels if you want and judicious
cut confetti of hot country pepper,
rub all this in with clean bare hands.

Your efforts will return to you
as aromas of contentment, harbingers of feasting
and well-being on Sunday afternoon.

I learned how to prepare Sunday dinners
the August when my father was found to be housing
agressive cells of destruction within him,

cells which were even now massing for the final
battle against his system, which they would win
in the closing days of the Advent season.

'Put the peas on after breakfast,' my mother said,
turning her domain, the kitchen, over to me
so that she could become his nurse at the end.

Their cooking requires close careful attention,
no long water will do, just enough to cover
and cook them till they sink to the bottom.

Then add enough water to buoy them again.
It's a game, this cooking of the peas.
Sometimes you allow them to cook down

until they almost burn. It is that cooked-down
near-burned state which produces that taste
of redeemed and rescued richness.

Repeat this boiling process over and over
until the hard red legumes soften.
Some of them will break open early

provided you do not cook them with salt.
The salt you add later when all peas have softened.
Flavor them again with more pressed garlic pearls.

Add the stripped length of stalks of escallion
pounded to release the onion brother juices.
Now toss a fragrant bouquet of thyme

into the swirling red waters of the pot,
which is even now awaiting the wash,
the white tide of coconut milk.

This part of the Sunday dinner ceremony
in times earlier was conducted by my father,
who would be summoned to the kitchen

and handed the instruments for performing
this ritual. A hammer, a knife, an ice pick,
a dry coconut bristling with fibrous hairs,

a male coconut in need of a shave
whose one eye you pierced with the ice pick's tip
to release a cloudy white fluid.

My father pauses to pour the water
into a long-stemmed wine glass
and lifts it like a chalice to my mother's lips.

Then he turns from this tender holy
and gallant gesture and splits open
the head of the coconut with the hammer.

The shell of the coconut cracks loudly
and opens to reveal that inside its thick skull
it is cradling a lining of firm white meat.

My father uses the blade of the knife
to separate the flesh from the shell,
and then he symbolically dips

a jagged piece of coconut into sugar
and chews upon it. This signals
the ending of this high domestic ceremony.

The coconut flesh is gathered up
and grated, then squeezed through a strainer.
The thick milk is tempered with water.

You pour that then like a libation
upon the seasoned red bubbling water
which is now ready to receive the rice,

clean sifted, picked, and washed
of all foreign bodies and impurities
like small pebbles and chaff

which remind us that all this is the produce,
the bounty of the earth into which
my father is preparing to return.

They come together, this integration
of rice and peas steamed in coconut milk,
mixed together and left to settle down

into a combined state of readiness.
All the time the meat has been roasting,
issuing from its side bloody gravy juices.

Now they will be serving her bland
hospital food, spiceless meat, mashed potatoes
accompanied by pastel vegetables.

This pale repast will be attended
by a nervous mound of red gelatin
and an eye cup of anemic ice cream.

They will encourage her to eat this
and to be thankful upon this Sunday
that at eighty-five she still lives.

For somedays she can only feed
upon an essential mixture, an imitation
plasma of salt sugar and water

dripping into her veins through a long
winding serpentine tube.
Over and over I watch for signs

that hearts are softening
that hard things are breaking open
that in the end it will all come together

like the Sunday dinner rice and peas.
As I pray for your soul's safety Mother,
as I pray for your blessed release.

Turn Thanks to Miss Mirry

Turn thanks to Miss Mirry
ill-tempered domestic helper who hated me.
She said that she had passed through hell bareheaded
and that a whitening ash from hell's furnace

had sifted down upon her and that is why she gray early.
Called me 'Nana'. Nanny's name I have come to love.
She twisted her surname Henry into Endry
in her railing against the graceless state of her days.

She was the repository of 400 years of resentment
for being uprooted and transplanted, condemned
to being a stranger on this side of a world
where most words would not obey her tongue.

She said that she came from 'Ullava'
in the parallel universe of Old Harbor.
She could not read or write a word in English
but took every vowel and consonant of it

and rung it around, like the articulated neck
of our Sunday dinner sacrificial fowl.
In her anger she stabbed at English, walked it out,
abandoned it in favor of a long kiss teeth,

a furious fanning of her shift tail, a series of hawks
at the back of her throat, a long extended elastic sigh,
a severing cut eye, or a melancholy wordless moaning
as she squatted over her wooden washtub soaping

our dirty clothes with a brown wedge of hard key soap.
To Miss Mirry who subverted the English language
calling Barbara, Baba; my father, Tata; who desiled her mind
that I was boofuttoo, a baffan and too rampify.

Who said pussbrukokonatinnadalikklegalnanayeye.
Miss Mirry versus English against the west
once assured me that for every sickness
there exists a cure growing in the bush.

I thank her for giving me a bath in her washtub
which she had filled with water heated
in a kerosene tin and in it she had strewed
the fringed leaves of the emancipation tamarind.

I turn thanks for the calming bath
that she gave to me which quelled effectively
the red itching measles prickling my skin.
As she sluiced the astringent waters over me

she was speak-singing in a language
familiar to her tongue which rose unfettered
up and down in tumbling cadences, ululations
in time with the swift sopping motion of her hands,

becoming her true self
in that ritual bathing, that song.
Turn thanks now to Miss Mirry
African bush healing woman.

Turn Thanks to Grandmother Hannah

My grandmother Hannah aspired to sanctity
through the domestic vocation of laundering
the used, soiled vestments of the clergy
into immaculate and unearthly brightness.

She would wash, starch and smooth them
like the last few feet of the road to heaven
with a heavy self-heater iron, its belly blazing
with the harnessed energy of the coals of hell.

Every clergyman in St Elizabeth's parish
would seek out her cleansing service.
Reclaiming that which seemed marked
for perdition was Hannah's holy gift.

Wine-stained altar cloths, once-chaste white albs
would rejoice, spotless, transfigured
to stand, redeemed under the resurrecting
power of grandmother Hannah's hands.

To be perfect in whatsoever you are called to do
is counted in heaven as sincere prayer.
My father's mother prayed through
laundering the garments used in temple service.

To my grandmother with the cleansing power
in her hands, my intention here is to give thanks
on behalf of any who have experienced within
something like the redemption in her washing.

Love Song for Great-Grandmother Leanna

With emancipation you married
a stout free Guinea man.
In your lawful estate
you cultivated ribbon cane.

On your paid-for property
wheeled your private sugar mill O.
You reaped from a deep grove
of fragrant allspice pimento.

You fanned your ripe berries
out upon your raised and wide barbecue.
For a wedding gift he gave you
a tall-flanked gray mule.

You rode upon it like a backra missus,
sidesaddle or astride depending on the day.
Sidesaddle days were Sundays
you cantered into Lucea to social soirees.

You descended from the mule's height
in one swift fluid movement.
And if someone too familiar should forget
themself and call out, 'Whoa Leanna'

you would turn and rebuke them,
'Say remember do, it is now Mrs Buddle to you.'

Aunt Rose's Honey Advice

My aunt Rose told me
that it is always good
for lovers to keep honey
mixed in with their food.

'Keep it around the house
at all times,' she said.
Replace slick butter
with pure honey on bread.

Feed it to your love
from a deep silver spoon.
Throw open the curtains
draw free honey from the moon.

Use it to lend a gold glow
to wan lustreless skin.
Fold it into honey cakes,
drizzle it into honey drinks.

Add a satin honey glaze
to the matte surface of everydays.
Voices sing polished
with honey's burnishing.

Shall we then beloved
become keepers of bees,
invite an entire colony
of workers, drones and a queen

to build complex
multicelled wax cities
near our home by the sea?
Would that mean that salt

would be savoring
through our honey?
And you say, 'What of it?'
and give me a kiss

flavored with honey
and sea-salt mix.
Integrated honey you say.
Kiss me again is what I say

because the salt in that kiss
could be the sting from old tears
and we need to make up
for all our honeyless years.

Domestic Incense

Just then, in that early afternoon,
I wanted to be that simple woman
who had cooked you Saturday soup

using all golden foods. Bellywoman
pumpkin, yellow yams, sweet potato,
carrots and deep ivory bones of beef.

I would bear it to you in an enamel bowl,
the smell of fragrant thyme and pimento
would waft, domestic incense, as I go.

How the hot Scotch Bonnet pepper
would issue its flavor through
the ripened walls of its own skin

but because like our love its seeds
can scorch, I'd be careful to remove it
before it cooked itself into breaking.

Signals from the Simple Life

A red cloth
tight around
her brow
and he knows
she is being
cleansed now
by the tides
of the moon.

White napkin
folded
over her sex
at death

is signal
to interfering spirits
she is done
with the ways of the flesh.

A poor man
wears new gloves
on his wedding day
to say
his hands
are clean.
This is
his new beginning.

This Is My Father's Country

I.

Yet when he died he did not own
one square inch of this rich red earth.
His body is interred in the churchyard
at Half Way Tree, far from his birthplace

eighty-seven miles from the wintergreen hills
of Malvern, the land his mother used to own,
well-fruited land, with the bearing Julie mango
tree, his navel string coiling at the roots.

My father's birthright was robbed
by a man whose intention it was
to store up much treasure here on earth.
A fox-name man stole my father's red land.

Sly Russell, you caught her in dry season.
Every crop that year had come to fail.
You caught Grandmother in the dry season,
her son sick with a fever there was no name for.

Grandmother, who never took her business
to strangers, in distress gave her land papers
to Russell to hold in exchange for a small sum,
six pounds to go and doctor her son.

The land papers stuck to Russell's fingers
and Grandmother received poor justice
when she appealed to King George
and his cohorts at Black River Courthouse.

Her only recourse was to petition
St Elizabeth, 'St Elizabeth come and see
this woman's dying trial, how I am left
with no red land of my own to walk upon,

to walk upon and raise my dumb animals,
to cultivate my crops, to will to my son.
I will lay down and die and be buried
under land that is not my own.

St Elizabeth, make tiefing Russell unable
to take my children's birthright with him.
May they use it as a loose red blanket
to cover him in his suit of cedar board.

St Elizabeth pray for my generations.
St Elizabeth please pray for my children's
children, pray for all of us who are not able
to store up treasures here on earth.

St Elizabeth, you who changed
the bread of the poor into roses
and then converted the roses
into the bread of the poor again,

grant us consoling strength
to bear our wounds and losses
and transform our sufferings
like the bread and the roses.'

II.

This is my father's country
and of late I have been thinking
how the burnished copper of his skin
could mean that he was Amerindian.

And as I write this I swear I see him smiling.

Like Arawak, my father did not come to stay.
His temper blazed sudden like bamboo fire
to be quickly dispersed by the wind
no traces of bitterness remaining.

My father of the tribe who came singing.

The earth is red here on the Pedro Plains
veils of rain mist shroud the trees, vapor
like winding sheets around Spur Tree Hill.
I hear now my spirit father, raconteur,

tell how it could take nights and days
for trucks to ascend these treacherous slopes.
How a Fargo would roll back like Sisyphus's stone
until the driver and sidemen effected the system,

called the cotching of the wheel. Advance a little,
cotch it with a stone, the recommended
way of advancement over any treacherous road.
Beloved, all the way here the roads ran red.

We cotched wheels, we stopped and waited,
eating of the round loaf, watching the waters
drench the fields, parched and unaccustomed
to wet they swallow hard and drink too fast.

In these parts, farmers have been known
to set straw traps to catch the morning dew.
In that way they moisten the roots of escallion
thyme, onion, potato, peas and sweet cassava.

Irrigation by grace and cultivation through
perseverance. Now for our coming, abundance.
Today there is torrential, overflowing blessing.
From my father's country drive away all drought.

The sight of your clean hands
breaking the bread
is turning my heart inside out.

My sweet-foot father could dance you see,
my nightingale-throat father could sing,
wind and string instruments obeyed him.

Here is a rude song he taught me
a ribald ditty, about the false candy
found by the village simpleton
and sung to one Bredda Manny.

Bredda Manny o mi fine a candy
Bredda Manny o mi fine a candy
dash it wey you nasty bitch
you nasty bitch, a puss shit.

Compose now a song for my father,
a man with well-shaped feet,
high-arched insteps for a man.
My father Marcus was a dandy.

A clean man who changed his shirts
often
Of Sea Island cotton in the Tower Isle
style
stood screened upon a background of white,

red-seamed Policemen upon point duty.
At regular intervals spring coconut trees,
recurring royally in between these
is the regal tower motif.

III.

They say that if you dream your father
and he does not speak that is an ill omen.
And I dream my father, he does not speak,
he does not speak, there is no need.

He smiles so and the room is filled
with stillness, high transcendent peace.
One Christmas I spent in New York alone
my father appeared to me on Dry Harbor Road.

He burst through the doors of the funeral home
and rapidly ascended the fire escape
then hovered as a bright ball of light
illuminating my solitary actions at evening.

He hovered outside in the snow
glowing over the music issuing out the window,
he and I serenaded by his favorite singer,
Harry Belafonte, crooning 'Jamaica Farewell'

and 'Shenandoah' and 'Sleep Late My Lady Friend'.

My Uncle

When my uncle died
he had daughters and sons
enough to bear his coffin
sufficient to lay him out.

One was a carpenter.
He built a fine casket
planed it from the trunk
of a fragrant cedar tree

that grew high as if heading
up to heaven ahead of uncle
lofty in his front yard
for the best part of a century.

One was a stone mason.
He constructed the vault.
While he was underground
he smoothed out a second tomb

for the pious wife of my uncle
who to this day still lives
on the nourishment pressed
from thin bible leaves.

His daughters, fine seamstresses,
lined his coffin with purple.
They washed and dressed him
in a serge suit of dark blue.

He'd cut and stitched it himself.
He was a tailor and farmer
with a gift in his hands
for good fit and perfect lucea yams.

His family fed all who came
to help them mourn
with the flesh of his goats
and ground provisions of his land.

I dreamt I saw my uncle
entering the Jubilee pavilion of Kings.
Osiris weighed his heart against a feather
and his heart was not found wanting.

The Sleeping Zemis

He kept the zemis under his bed for years
after the day he came upon them in a cave
which resembled the head of a great stone god,
the zemis placed like weights at the tip of its tongue.

Arawaks had hidden them there when they fled,
or maybe the stone god's head was really a temple.
Now under his bed slept three zemis,
wrought from enduring wood of ebony.

The first was a man god who stood erect, his arms
folded below his belly. The second was a bird god
in flight. The third was fashioned in the form
of a spade, in the handle a face was carved.

A planting of the crops zemi,
a god for the blessing of the corn,
for the digging of the sweet cassava
which requires good science

to render the white root safe food.
And over the fields the john crows wheel
and the women wait for the fishermen
to return from sea in boats hollowed from trees.

Under his bed the zemis slept.
Where were they when Columbus
and his men, goldfever and quicksilver
on the brain, came visiting destruction?

Man god we gave them meat, fish and cassava.
Silent deity we mended their sails, their leaking
ships, their endless needs we filled even with
our own lives, our own deaths.

Bird god, we flew to the hills,
their tin bells tolling the deaths
of our children, their mirrors
foreshadowing annihilation to follow.

Spade god we perished.
Our spirits wander wild and restless.
There was no one left to dig our graves,
no guides to point us the way to Coyaba.

He turned them over to the keepers of history,
they housed them in glass-sided caves.
Then he went home to sleep without the gods
who had slumbered under his bed for years.

Africa on the Mind Today

Over the wall the workmen chant
riding the rhythm hammer on nail
beating out a one-drop that will not
be forgotten after four hundred years.

Rounding a corner in Green Island
by the restless cobalt sea at evening
a line of young men run in formation
like warriors at the hunt of the lion.

Africa on the mind today.
The workmen drumming over the wall
call to Miriam singing Sangoma
sing a 'do not destroy' for Winnie Mandela.

Sing a Bide-Up for Wole Soyinka
say, Abeocuta rock of our foreparents stay.
Strength of Guinea women on our mother's side,
Africa rest, Abeocuta abide.

The Mango of Poetry

I read a book
about the meaning of poetry.
The writer defines it as silence,
then breaks the lines

to construct ideas
about the building of bridges,
the reconciliation of opposites.
I'm still not sure what poetry is.

But now I think of a ripe mango
yellow ochre niceness
sweet flesh of St Julian,
and all I want to do

is to eat one from the tree
planted by my father
three years before the sickness
made him fall prematurely.

The tree by way of compensation
bears fruit all year round
in profusion and overabundance
making up for the shortfall

of my father's truncated years.
I'd pick this mango with a cleft stick,
then I'd wash it and go to sit
upon the front wall of our yard.

I would not peel it all back
to reveal its golden entirety,
but I would soften it by rolling
it slowly between my palms.

Then I'd nibble a neat hole
at the top of the skin pouch
and then pull the pulp
up slowly into my mouth.

I'd do all this while wearing
a bombay-colored blouse
so that the stain of the juice
could fall freely upon me.

And I say that this too would be
powerful and overflowing
and a fitting definition
of what is poetry.

To Mr William Wordsworth, Distributor
of Stamps for Westmoreland

The host of golden flowers at my feet
were common buttercups not daffodils,
they danced and swayed so in the breeze
though overseer thorns were planted among them.

Still, it was a remarkable show of sorts
which opened my eye, the inward one,
which once opened enabled me to see
the overflowing bounty of my peoples' poverty.

Sir, did you pass my great-grandmother?
Like you she lived in Westmoreland,
she rode upon a great gray mule,
she could not read or write, she did not buy stamps.

But great-grandmother was a poet
who wrote her lyrical ballads on air,
scripted them with her tongue
then summoned them to return to her book of memory.

She never did arrange them
the exact same way twice
but they were her powerful overflow
recollected in tranquility, sir, what she chanted was poetry.

Great-grandmother was Black Betty's daughter,
sister to fool fool Rose, distant cousin
to Betty Foy's idiot boy. Laughingstock
of the West Country, of no degree, she spoke funny.

But, sir, whenever she would sing
even the solitary reaper's voice was stilled
as her wild mystic chanting issued
over the cane brakes and hills. Only Keats's nightingale

could compete with her guinea griot style.
But she was not in any contest
for the fittest of the fit, she had just come
with her wild ways to enchant with her riddling lyrics.

Mr Wordsworth, I am not buying any stamp
to post a letter to my great-grandmother.
She is a denizen of the spirit world like you
so I am asking you when you pass her there, to tell her

that I collected up all her songs and poems
from where they fell on banana trash.
The binding ones on the star apple tree,
the ones hidden like pound notes under her coir mattress.

I rescued them, rat-cut Blue Mountain coffee,
the ratoon and dunder ones, refuse and trash
of the sugarcane, the ones they call broken
and indecent, patois, bungo, words for bondage and shame.

And I've written them down for her,
summoned them to stand, black-face type
against a light background, Mr Wordsworth.
Please tell Miss Leanna her poems are now written down.

Country, Sligoville

I arise and go with William Butler Yeats
to country, Sligoville
in the shamrock green hills of St Catherine.

We walk and palaver by the Rio Cobre
till we hear tributaries
join and sing, water songs of nixies.

Dark tales of Maroon warriors,
fierce women and men
bush comrades of Cuchulain.

We swap duppy stories, dark night doings.
I show him the link of a rolling calf's chain
and an old hige's salt skin carcass.

Love descended from thickets of stars
to light Yeats's late years with dreamings
alone I record the mermaid's soft keenings.

William Butler, I swear my dead mother
embraced me. I then washed off my heart
with the amniotic water of a green coconut.

In December Sally water will go down
to the Sally gardens with her saucer
and rise and dry her weeping orbs.

O to live, Inisfree, in a house of wattle and daub.

Antoinette Cosway Explains

It was always this way.
A morning breeze passing
could bruise my cheek.
The white zest of jasmine
trailed indoors by the night wind
would settle itself upon my skin
then conduct its essence down
into my blood, causing my body
to swarm and my head to spin.

Everything that I saw
was stirred up so,
wild cocoa leaves
became at once menacing masks.
Helaconia blooms were totemic staffs.
The inverted bell-mouth of angel trumpet
flowers would come to resemble
the turned-down cups of bitter port
drunk by fallen angels.

It was always so.
Standing in sunshine a cooler sun
would appear and direct its rays down
to render me cold.
The warm waters of the bathing pool
never refreshed but chilled me.
Sent me shivering to sit
on a warm white stone
which at my touch turned cool.

And the stone-heart girl,
the stone-heart girl
stole my good dress,
my friendship.
my bright pennies.
I hear counter-music
under all music,
no matter how they play
piano, piano.

I hear the streeling of Gypsy fiddles
of Gaelic choirs keening burial songs
just when the same destructive man
(he comes in different disguises
but he is the same man)
places his slow hand low
upon the small of my back and then
tilts my head back to begin again
to go-round go-round dance of death.

The Gypsy in the Russian Tea Room

The Gypsy in the Russian Tea Room
nests in a banquette like a fat firebird
with brocaded plumage. Her scarlet
and black tasseled scarf drips silk feathers
upon the figured carpet. At the center
of her forehead is fixed a silver eye,
the soothsayer's outward sign.

This man and woman in the Russian
Tea Room could tell the Gypsy
tales about cataclysm and misfortune.
Advise her how to dodge the fallout
from exploding planets and malevolent
constellations. They could sell her charms
to protect her when the conjunction of Mars

and treacherous women and venal men
means take low and keep silent, till scorpion
planets consume themselves. They do not want
their fortunes told. She has already bought
hers from the wandering wine-seller. His was
concealed in the purple grapes upon which he feeds.
Their fortune is to drink the mixed wine of destiny.

Vincent and the Orient

The blackbird in the bougainvillea bush
brushes against the powder blue sky.
The carnelian froth of the flowering tree,
and the way that this picture
framed itself inside my window,

makes me remember again Vincent
and the Orient he would imitate,
japonaiserie, white-petaled trees
set spare in an Eastern landscape.
They are not my favorite; dearer to me

are those in which familiar things turn
transcendent. Golden cornfields
shimmy like blonde dancing girls,
hips rolling, abandoned, fecund.
The red turban of a zouave's uniform

pulses like a live internal organ.
Strange how I never meditate upon
the harsh details of his death
but see instead the glory of his gift
for transforming elementary things

through patience and careful seeing
past all obvious appearances
down to where the whirling spirits
flash primal pigments, creating
images, sensuous, duende, amazing.

Max Ernst Painting

This floating woman without a head
her left arm missing.
The woman wearing one translucent
pink stocking
levitates in a blue space, rags and feathers
shudder from vents in the ceiling.

Someone just threw a stone at her.
See it drop to the base of the picture.
Maybe it was the stone that decapitated her.
There is a conical red stroke falling
from an indigo mass below
where the rags and feathers blow.

This woman with her head gone
she is partly a nun, partly naked maja.
Her left arm connected to her heart
grew weary of constantly reaching out
and returning empty it fell into the sea.

About her head. You know how I said
it was severed by a stone?
I suspect it was thrown by someone
who had no sins they wished to speak of.

The Jerboa of John Dunkley

A jerboa logo on shoe polish tin
leaps its way into Barber's vision,
it settles into his dream life
and becomes his own icon.

Barber what a razor's edge
you walked, walking your razor
through the curled lamb's wool
of the head of the Negro.

As you barber you are called to stain
your chair with primodial images.
Jerboa dancing in the barber mirror
made you shut up shop that day

it yielded hairs for brush bristles
and you covered the canvas with gray.
'When I paint I take a walk,' you confessed
to the keeper of dreams, Philip,

and then you showed him your painting
of a lone being in the Bog Walk gorge
observing a dark horse and buggy
go past rocky roads of miry clay.

Draw deep from your palette sombre,
pure palette brooding chiaroscuro.
Dark greens and silver, muted
like the voice of the sing-slow Barber.

Down the winding rabbit hole
through the door of no return
Barber reclaims original landscape,
blue road ribbons to Port of Al Mina.

Marsupial jerboa leaps from shoe polish tin
blue rabbit roots at banana tree
when Barber takes a walk down the road
of captured collective memory.

Hungry Belly Kill Daley

I fancied that I could paint
a still life with food,
and my rendering of victuals
would be so good
that I could reach into the canvas
and eat and fill my belly.

111

Cadmium yellow could spread
butter impasto over white lead
or a brown loaf baked of sienna.
Scarlet and vermilion, the wine
would flow, otaheiti apple
is a deep, dark, rose madder.

If I could fill my hungry belly
with painted wine and bread
but they shock my visions from my head
at Bellevue, where Louis Q. Bowerbank
sends madmen or black men mad enough
to think that we could be artists in 1940.

To Become Green Again and Young

In Rio de Janeiro
they go at midnight
to welcome the new year.

Fresh in white garments
bearing white candles
they assemble by the sea

to toss old year's errors
griefs and mistakes
into the accepting waves.

Begin again fresh and new
when the year turns to become
green again and young.

Would there was a body of water
deep and wide enough
for the errors of some of us.

Arctic, Antarctic, Atlantic, Indian, Pacific
Caribbean Sea, Atlantic Ocean
where our ancestors drowned.

There is a spirit nation
under the ocean. May its citizens plead
for our recovery and redempion.

Midnight at the close of this year,
ancestral spirits urge us
to entrust our sorrows to the sea.

God a Me

Tide wash me out of the river
sweep me up onto the bank.

I was swimming in sync
so with the live currents

of the big rivers, one hundred
rivers of this green island.

Now here I am beached
but still breathing.

They say I'm the only one
who can live so

outside of the water culture
where fish flourish and grow.

Fish out of water
God a me

Fish live on land
God a me

Slightly amphibian
God a me

My name itself a prayer
God a me

On land I breathe uneasy
but still breathe though

until the tides of mercy
pull me

back into
the flow.

God a me.

Sometimes on a Day Such as This

Sometimes on a day such as this
after four or five hours
of medicinal silence
I am eased to this place.

I return home to myself,
clean, stripped. I enter
through the high blue door
of myself. I sit.

Within this chamber
of myself
loving you is as high a pleasure
as I will ever get.

See now my expanded self
grow many arms,
like a Hindu deity they issue
from my sides.

On cue, connected, I glow.
I become a living chandelier
swinging slightly with delight
because now you will pass beneath me

and one of my many lit fingers
will thoughtfully circle the crown
of your head.
And it will glow, halo.

Inside me I am never ashamed,
I am whole and me.
One thousand errors, transmuted
errors, now become iron

fed back into my blood.
I can hear a strong coursing
through my veins in the silence.
In the silence my blood runs

like the Tiber or the Black River.
My body contains a body
of strong surging water.
And I can hear it

sometimes on a day such as this
when I return home to me
after five hours or so
of medicinal silence.

A Bed of Mint

A bed of mint
beneath the window
of the room where we sleep
will render the morning air
sharp and sweet.

I'd turn to you in my sleep
half out of dreams
murmuring 'Whose bed
is it that smells of mint?'
'Ours' you will whisper.

Then we will roll over
like the waves and wake
to draw tea from the source
springing beneath the window.
Lying sweet and ital to each other.

I Know I Never Lose You

I know now that I never lose you.
Look how you came calling today
as thoughtful Sunday afternoon rain.

You in the making of the escoveitch,
onions, pepper, pimento, oil and vinegar,
for you all rejoice together.

Shiver the air then.
Combined condiments of praise,
you numinous in everdays.

Now strewn over the fatness
of fried butter fish,
behold bright thanksgiving garnish.

Like salt stirred evenly
into smooth food,
your presence permeates everything good.

Like oil in a cloth or dye
your substance imparted
changes the texture, the color of things.

You in all things, O everything,
all atoms saturated then
with your unction grace and presence.

Angel of Dreamers

Angel, ever since I come back here trying to reopen this dream
shop I get so much cuss-cuss and fight down, these merchants
don't want me to prosper in this town.

Seraph mine you supervised and trained me, inspected my goods
declared it celestial first quality. But cherubim what a cherubam
since I land.

I set up my shop in this big sprawling bazaar, central, to draw
them from near and from far. Well the first thing that I notice all
around and about me

is other sellers living in fear and under necromancy. Every morning they get up they squeezing lime to cut and clear and all I
using is the power of prayers.

Some consulting with D lawrence (darkness) writing down my
name on parchment. Some have taken to attacking my name in
malcrafted, lopsided imitations of my creations

all because of bad mind. Angel, if you see the spoil-goods they
peddle as dreamwares. Chuh, I leaving them to count the pro-
ceeds from their bankruptcy sales.

For seraph, you should see how I fix up my shop, nobody round
here ever see a shop fix up like that. When I throw open the doors
not even the most bad-minded

117

could come out with their usual naysaying, carping and fault finding. For I have painted the walls in a deep evergreen, and all around the cornices and along the ceiling

I have picked out the subtle patterns in the mouldings in the indigo of discernment so what was hidden has now become clear, illuminate, and prominent.

Along the walls I have placed some long low cane-seat couches. The cushions all covered in the lavender of lignum vitae. It is there that dreamers sit and drink rosemary tea.

On the floor I dropped a rug of lagoon blue with feathers floating free on its surface, and if you look long and your eye is clear, you see schools of goldfish swimming down there.

And my extraordinary dreamshop was opened with no fanfare, not one high official, Pharisee or Tappanaris was there. I just threw open the doors and sat there quietly

till some dreamseeker pass by and noticed me. Someone well-parched from too much hard-heart life, they look up and see my sign a crescent moon with a single star fixed

and dreamseller lettered in font Gazelle, lower case, sans serif. And so they stumble in weary, having tried various health schemes and bush medicines and ask me for a dream.

As soon as they ask me I go to work like Attar, the darwish chemist, my ancestor. In a clean crucible I mix the fallout from stars and the fragrant dyestuff of roses.

I add to this, then, various elements for the restoration of lost shining. Only one or two hearts that have lived too long in the dark professed dissatisfaction with the dream they bought.

But most of the ones who acquire them always come back in to report how acquiring their dream has alchemically changed and altered their way of seeing and being.

They say to all visitors, 'Come see this dream I have received from the seller in the bazzar, godchild of Ghazali, student of Attar, the love child of Rumi and Asi Itra.

One of the ancient keepers of dreams and songs, great grand-daughter of a psalmist and griot Guinea woman. They say if you deserve one of these she will mix you one

to quicken your hopes and tune your heart to hear songs of bliss. All she takes for payment is sincerity and red roses.' I have received many referrals in this way.

The ones who acquire these dreams are inspired to light candles of understanding which illuminate all they do thereafter with a clear pervasive shining.

I am writing this to you seated at the shop door where the simurgh, that cinnabar talisman of a bird, has just flown in and perched upon one of the bunches of wine-fruit

which hang ripe from the ceiling. Sometimes ground doves fly in and Barbary doves too. Let me attempt to describe the transcendent Barbary dove song for you.

*

The Transcendent Song as Taught by a Passing Tuareg Woman

A Tuareg woman passing once taught me a song.
It was really a series of intricate notes
urgently sounded, like the fast-forward call
of a rising flock of Barbary doves.

The song, if correctly and effectively done,
can lift me up to a cool place
above the burning chamber of the sun.
The woman said it is the transcendent song

known only to the ones like us.
I caught the song and held it.
I feel it is not wise to use it too frequently.
Just so, I have learned to save it for unbearable days.

119

First a series of fluttering notes
then a long low fluting coo.

Then a series of fast-forward notes
till there occurs a wild breakthrough.

Then a joyful, joyful gurgling
like a full-throttle rain replenished stream

and after that it's just pure sweet cooing.

*

The only way that I have been able to withstand
the undermining efforts of the other sellers
is to sound this transcendent song.

Until I see you face-to-face, I ask you to pray that God grant
me celestial insurance from the arsonist efforts
of the job-lot sellers.

A Quartet of Daffodils

I think it must be spring
because yesterday morning on Spadina
there was an Indian woman walking
wrapped in maximum eight yards of sari cloth.
It was sheer and a luminous color
like the nectar of pressed apricots.

A red dot punctuated the center of her brow,
like a small and urgent point of energy
had found its way to the surface of her skin
and jeweled, or a drop of blood, it was gleaming.
I think it must be spring because
there is not a host but a quartet of daffodils

sprung up in the front yard of Gore Vale.
They stand not straight but bowed over so.
I think that they had a hard time making it out
of their frozen birthplace inside the earth.
Nevertheless, they are here and have come in first.
The runners-up are the crocuses.

But the evergreen never went under,
it just spread its branches taut and took the worst
that winter had to offer. Do not go under
and one day you may be crowned with evergreen.
This year is my third spring, the third time
that I have been witness to the cycle of the seasons.

Where I am born, there is no such thing,
seasons just shift over a bit to accommodate
the one following. Our winters bring tangerines
and pimento winds. Bless now death, resurrection,
the peculiar ascension of ice falls finally away.

I think it must be spring now because today
I feel so tender, like all early things budding.
And even if I am coming in exhausted,
bowed, bent, drawn, and yellow-skinned
like my very first quartet of daffodils
I know now that this is undeniably spring.

Coo Coo

Coo coo, fool fool.
Hear what that old man bird with the rusty chestnut belly
and guttural call rasps at you. He is declaring you fool fool.

From the Parakeet in the garden that Simon Peter heard
to the parson Johncrow with the distinguishing white feather,

the little grass quit and the quit with yellow shoulder
all of them feel they can jump up and dub you, fool fool.

Ringillidae finch, chattering sparrows and grosbeaks,
follow-line birds of dull plumage who nest in cavities

and eat of accumulated insect droppings, convene conference
to discuss what they term your extraordinary appearance.

How you appeared first as ground dove taking low, observing
    how
the scissor-tail hummingbird cut through gravity and
    accomplished

flight mastery. Fly backwards or straight ahead and even hover,
winged helicopter, on the same spot when mark time is needed.

They write you off as birdbrain when you were trying to fly
and the killy and hawk and the mockingbirds laughed at you.

Your father himself, wise as pattoo, took you to one side
and whispered, 'Do not be overfriendly with the John Crow
    family.'

What made you ignore him and decide to fly with vultures,
chicken-hawks, back-stabbing petchary and carrion-eating
    company?

Rufoustal flycatcher big Tom fool, his little brother, sad flycatcher
little Tom Fool, want to come and duck their muddy heads.

O cavity dwellers laying heavily spotted eggs (and want to call
    them
poems). Even they feel that they can call you fool fool.

Once you imitated the Sarah bird and lived in the hills in search
of elevation, frequented forests and made your nest feather-lined

but you lacked the necessary steel gray plumage to be of the
    tyrant
flycatcher kind. So you dropped down to the plains to regroup.

And dance bird, Ivy Baxter told you that Xamayca is a land older
than most, that it is in fact a pointed finger, a raised shoulder

of Atlantis under the sea, where twenty billion drowned birds
and drowned dreams lie, with lost poets, sing sad aye coo coo.

You need to know that you are of the species Trochilidae,
and if you live content to be ground dove and come-follow-me

and choose for confidantes labba mouth sharp-billed kestrels
and fire hawks, why wonder that your emerald plumage is
    singed?

So once more, Trochilidae of the family of 319 species, you have
ranged from far Alaska to the sheer heights of the Andes

where you fly in the form of wide-winged cousin to condor
and small up yourself over Cuba as Ave, size of a bumblebee.

Bill and tongue, tongue and bill, upcurved, downcurved, slender,
    slim
sight up your sign, the half moon sickle with the fixed star within.

Bill of sword which will cut through sword of treacherous king.
Bill to gather, such a gathering, of noisome insects self-promoting.

Gather nettles, then turn to draw the sweet honey nectar, gather
nectar and eat insects too, the sweet and the bitter both nourish
    you.

Dazzle and dazzle them, wear your garments iridescent like flying
precious stones. Aye sapphire, and topaz in flight and emerald
    lustre

to astonish and illuminate. When they gather to study your vocal
chords in order to imitate your taffeta laugh, make the percussive

click and sound the Om, with the whir-beating of your wings.
Flash and fly when the swarms of wannabees come, it is meet

to lower your body's temperature and draw down into your
necessary reserve, there to go silent till the sun stuns them

with the gold of enlightenment. Who except Farid'du din Attar,
The Rose's essence, can you call to conference and Parliament?

Bringing the Wild Woman Indoors

You'd cleansed yourself with astringent blue soap lather
rinsed your skin in a baptism of pure rainwater

robed yourself in starched garments of white
turned your face upward to catch the light

and then she came in. Disheveled and weeping,
her hair tangled, her half-hemmed dress trailing.

She had mauve-stained shadows under her eyes
like the solitaire had brushed its wings there all night.

'Instead of an attic,' she says, 'you have forced me to live
under the house-bottom with your discarded things.

Me, the one who stood sentinel outside your doorway
while you cultured the new voice, the new poetry.

Who was it ripped the face off the devil when
he tried to petrify you down in the stone gardens?

I am the one who masked for you for years so
they believed that you were half-witted and slow

and because of that they chat you, laughed at you
and left you alone, allowing you to decode the news

brought by the viridian-plumaged bird who flew down
at night from the Ashanti aviary in Nanny Town.'

And as she spoke you saw yourself in her, the wild woman,
your true sister. And you say, 'Thank you for being the mad one,

the wild heart, the crazy woman, the Accompong Nanny warrior.'
And that's when you brought her to live inside with you forever.

The Revival Song of the Wild Woman

The wild woman will never let you go back to living alone.
She has you in her control, leading you helplessly astray,
preaching her don't-care philosophy, 'No matter what the people
of the world may say.'

And she tells you now to go with her to where our music is buried,
and sing loud revival songs that will waken the dead
singers and players of instruments who sell out Don Drummond's
and Bob Marley's heritage.

This morning she caught your attention early, told you to dress
in fiery red, and you who have been keeping your life colors
in the range between muted and pastel are now garbed
in brimstone red

with an infinite number of polka dot eyes all over so you
are now able to see behind, before, above and all around you.
And she is telling you to take a bus up to August Town to where
Alexander Bedward dipped them.

And she says that you are to throw stones in Hope River and
        trouble
the water, to signal the time of the coming of a new shepherd.
        Then
take a country bus down to Half Way Tree and go and stand
by the fountain.

There you are to testify freely and not worry what your enemies
        say
for they will never live long enough to vanquish you, therefore do
your unconquered dance right there, your dance of David trump
and wheel o'rock steady

accompanied by tumbling tambourines and a funde drum and a
        kete
drum and a silver horn to blow the bad-minded down. Yes,
the wild woman is in ascendancy today, summoning the freed
        soul
in you to testify and pray.

To wear brimstone red and to wrap your head and to move
    seamlessly
up and down between the worlds of spirit and sense, like the
    flight
of the mystical dove. And if your mother won't come, and if your
father won't come

Peace and Love I leave with you, Peace and Love,
and if your mother won't come, and if your father won't come
Peace and Love I leave with you, Peace and Love.

Close to You Now

Close to you now
I talk at the evening sky.
Maybe that is where your heart is,
your chest all decorated with stars
and the keen scythe blade
of the crescent moon.

Ever since I gave up telling to anyone
but you, I have become so filled
with love that I used to waste.
Now I confess to you straight.
I ask you questions. I sleep.
I speak the answers when I wake.

When I gave up walking
from door to door with my begging bowl
I became conscious that my bowl
had been always full of the fine gold wheat
which only the prayerful can see and eat.
And all the time I was living on leftovers.

I lie in my bed and cry out to you.
I cover myself with a humming tune spread
which says as it weaves itself

you, you and only you.
No one could ever sight up
the true intentions of this heart.

But ever since I stop explaining
I watch them blow past me like chaff.
Alone and silent now I hear again
the coded notes played by the rain
which dictated the first poems.
I want to walk across this green island

singing like the Guinea woman
showers, showers of blessing
until you cover my lips
and I go silent and still
and I will see your face
and want then for nothing.

Was it Legba She Met outside the Coronation Market?

Under the arch of the Coronation Market
she watches the crooked man approach.
He is a dromedary with a double hump,
one of muscle and cartilege, one a crocus bag sack
swollen with the rank weeds and fragrant leaves
of his travelling bush doctor's business.

He bends over and overlooks the child,
she can see the red-veined whites of his eyes
He leans backward and then falls into a trance
during which he removes his eye's white ball
and swallows it. It reappears in her palm, she returns
the white sphere, he swallows it and speaks prophecy.

Then he limps away with his halt legba walk.
But she is left at the crossroads hearing the call,
spirits assembled, casting their lots to decide
who will claim her voice and speak through it
the as yet untold half. Her mother returns, laden down
with ground provisions. The child is silent as the ball's
white weight levitates on the tip of her tongue.

I Am Weary of Winters Mother

I fear that I will stop strangers
in the snowlined street
to tell them 'My mother is dead.'

In a bookstore on Ash Wednesday
I saw a white-haired woman
with the sign of the cross on her forehead.

I am weary of all winters mother
winter within, winter without,
strict-fasting Ramadan, Lenten do-without.

Spending the Gold of Lovers

It was the same morning that the Blue Mountains
contracted and stamped themselves, imprimateur
across my forehead, I saw it happen in the mirror
as combed my hair.

Right after that words began to float from my lips,
words for which I had no meaning, like 'Lailah',
which means 'a night', and 'Ali' who later became
my rose seller.

128

Just then the rain of coins fell. Gold started pouring
from the vents in the ceiling. I gathered it up and that
is what I've been careless and wantonly spending
in my sojournings.

There was this man on the bus today inviting anyone
who so desired to come and freely dine with him.

'Anyone who wants to can come,' he said, 'I have money
I can pay.' I saw then that this same gold had rained
down upon him.

Just poured from the ceiling of his rented room,
filling his pockets so he could afford to be profligate,
ignoring the reasonable woman

cautioning 'save your money for a rainy day.'
'No,' he insisted, 'I can pay, I will pay
and whosoever will may come.'

About the Tamarind

Under strict dry conditions I can grow as high
as eighty feet and my open frame half as wide.
Then my trunk which yields a kind of timber
called by some the mahogany of Madeira
will become too substantial and stout for you
to wrap your short arms around.

My crown, a mass of fine light green foliage,
pinate leaves, which dip gracefully to shade you
fold in upon themselves at night, private.
I bloom small gold flowers which appear
to bleed the gold of guinea and the blood
drawn by the lash of slavery.

I am slow growing, rooted deep, resisting
breeze blow, hot air and hurricane winds.
I flourish even in rocky terrain with little or no
cultural attention. My cinnamon brown pods
grow in profusion, I bear long, I bear abundance
and Pharoahs ate of me.

Tamir Hindi the Persian poet chanted under my shade.
Rooted first in Africa, transplanted wherever
I can thrive, that is wherever there is sun of life.
I require his constant kiss in order to flourish.
His hot caresses I absorb and return in the form
of fire purifying, all-consuming.

Tamarindus Indica, native of Africa, from root
to leaftip, my every part has been employed
to meet human need. Consider how they eat
my flowers and leaves, roast my seeds, pound them
into paste for sizing. My fruit which is sometimes sour
can be sugared into tamarind balls, symbols of slavery.

Sometimes in alluvial soil I grow large and sweet,
that is in places where I am valued and needed.
Then I heal, refrigerant for fevers, I am laxative.
I work alone or can combine with juice of limes
or extrusion of bees, together we can cure
bilious digestive systems large as that of elephants.

I reduce swellings, loosen the grip of paralysis,
and return the drunken inebriated on illusion,
the cheap coarse wine of the world, to sobriety
perhaps to become one day truly drunk like me
with the wine unseen, which causes me to sway
so that the unannointed mock me.

In Africa they soak my bark with corn
and feed this to domestic birds in the belief
that if they stray or are stolen they will return.
In Asia, a little tamarind and coconut milk
is placed at the mouths of infants as their first drink,
the world's initial welcoming libation.

And the elephant's long memory is aided by the eating
of my bark and the pods, flesh and seeds of my fruit.
My leaves give soothing bush baths for rashes or the cut
of the tamarind whip. The correction and the cure
both come from me. There are people who claim
I am dwelling place of the spirit of rain.

I raise the temperature in my immediate vicinity
so the cold-hearted fear me. I will tell you now
why few plants grow wild beneath me and why
you should not use me as policetree to tether your horse.
Because I have not come to rule over, overpower
vanquish, conquer or constrain anyone.

I provide the mordant in dyes, burn me for charcoal
I rise as insense. My sapwood is pale and golden.
My heartwood though is royal purple and earth brown,
I am high and low all at once. Sour and sweet,
I came with the enslaved across the seas to bear for you
when force-ripe capricious crops fail.

I bear. Not even the salt of the ocean can stunt me.
Plant me on abiding rock or foaming restless waters.
Set me in burying grounds, I will shade the ancestors.
O bitter weed and dry-heart tree, wait for me to bow.
I hope you can wait. Rest in Peace, Arawaks.
I am still here, still bearing after 400 years.

For Love of Marpesa Dawn

Long summer vacation 1963
After seeing Black Orpheus
Garth Baker confessed his love
for the gorgeous Marpessa Dawn.

He had been going to Cross Roads
to see her at the State Theatre
and after some seven matinees
and at least two night shows

He was convinced that she
was his destiny. As soon as he
finished sixth form he was going
to take a banana boat to Brazil.

Once there, he'd slip past Cerebos
in the form of a massive-headed
wharf dog, and find his way to Rio
to meet Marpessa outside a theatre.

There he would serenade her
upon a lute, lyre, or box guitar
with a slow ska, a hard rocksteady
a sweetie-come-brush-me bossanova

Till she recognized him as Orpheus
returned from the underworld.
And we believed him. We were
willing to make that leap of faith

For we were were all misplaced beings
our true selves ripped from the world book
of myths. But Garth had found his identity
and he would be reunited with Eurydice.

one radiant Marpessa Dawn.

Outwaiting the Crazy Wolf Moon

In the North country the native people
call this the moon when wolves go crazy.
Here, they warn against gathering bamboo
and wiss at the time of the full moon's rising.

For that is when the chi-chi larvae swarm
in bamboo joints and wiss is alive with insects.
You will find that what you have gathered
is a bundle of useless sticks, sick with parasites.

It is wise to wait for the timely rise
of the verdigris moon called 'glad to be alive'.
Soon after will follow the one of new life.
The moon of pure silver which presides over

the melting of the ice, the earth as it thaws
and causes resurrection lilies to appear
defiant by hard walls of penitentiaries,
burst sudden from cracks in tombs

and bloom in the yards of faithful lovers
who bit their tongues and sucked salt
as they learned strict patience and outwaited
the mad moon of the crazy wolves.